BodyArt: People

by Carol Hauswald and Alice Maskowski

This BodyArt book is gratefully dedicated to:

David
Michael
Rainbow Tree Kids
Kristin

for their inspirations
and to:

Dan and Mike

for their dedication to our efforts.

Publisher: Roberta Suid

Editor: Beverly Cory

Cover Design: David Hale

Production: Susan Cronin-Paris

For a complete catalog, write to the address above.

ISBN 1-878279-42-4

Printed in the United States of America

9 8 7 6 5 4 3 2 1

CONTENTS

Introduction 4

Worries and Fears 7

Feeling Fine 17

Fabulous Families 33

Cheerful Chums 45

Crackerjack Communities 57

Going Global 67

INTRODUCTION

A handprint grass-seed planter . . .

A nightmare (horse) made from a child's handprint and decorated with scraps of yarn . . .

Cardboard shoe soles traced from parents' shoes and worn in an I'm-a-big-person march . . .

A child's coat-of-arms based on a handprint . . .

The pages that follow provide models and simple directions that will enable you and your children to produce these and scores of other artifacts relating to friends, family, community, and feelings. The projects grow from hands, fingers, feet, toes, and other body parts. You'll also find related crafts, songs, finger plays, games, snacks, and dramatic play activities that integrate all these resources into a whole-learning environment that fosters imagination and self-esteem.

Let's Celebrate People

This book's multi-sensory approach to learning focuses on six units about children and their place in the world:

Worries and Fears. No child is immune from scary dreams, thoughts of being lost, and other painful aspects of growing up. BodyArt projects—for example, projecting finger monsters on a wall—give children a sense of control over these anxieties. They also teach children they are not alone in facing frightening things.

Feeling Fine. The other side of the coin is affirming one's own unique being. In this unit, you'll find a variety of can-do activities ranging from I-like-me body tracing to singing silly songs. It's all part of what makes children feel good about themselves.

Fabulous Families. Family life is a delicate topic, especially these days when so many children live in non-traditional arrangements. BodyArt family activities, such as creating family-tree bulletin boards—are meant to help children recognize and accept their place in a loving family, whatever the form.

Cheerful Chums. A child's friendship circle is a vital extension of the family. With activities such as friendly handprint wrapping paper, this unit honors these special people that children choose to be close to.

Crackerjack Communities. A child's vision gradually expands outward, like ripples in a pond, into the community at large. Here, BodyArt activities—like making stop-and-go traffic signs—focus on special community helpers, as children imagine themselves in various roles.

Going Global. Finally, children enter the global village. Projects like ceremonial face masks introduce cultural diversity, while at the same time clarifying the essential similarities among people around the world. Though different on the surface, we are—at the core—mirror images of one another.

Literature Links

Each unit of *BodyArt: People* includes a list of picture-book read-alouds. They will awaken and sustain children's interest in language and in the subject matter covered. The books are sensitively written, beautifully illustrated, and age-appropriate.

These books make wonderful springboards into the units. Even better, many of them tie directly to specific BodyArt projects. For example, after making hand-based family trees, children will enjoy listening to *My Grandson Lew* or *Big Sister and Little Sister,* both by Charlotte Zolotow.

Another option is to use the books as follow-ups to BodyArt activities. The stories can inspire creative drama, puppetry, spontaneous games, child-drawn picture books, movement songs, and child-dictated stories—just a few of the activities that contribute to whole language.

The books are readily available through libraries and bookstores. Inexpensive paperback editions can often be purchased through children's book clubs. Two that we use frequently are:

The Trumpet Club
666 Fifth Avenue
New York, NY 10103

Scholastic, Inc.
730 Broadway
New York, NY 10003

Materials for the BodyArt Projects

The BodyArt projects require common arts and crafts supplies that most preschool centers and classrooms will already have on hand: nontoxic tempera or fingerpaint, crayons, washable markers, nontoxic glue, scissors, hole punchers, butcher paper, construction paper, rolls of colored bulletin board paper, and tagboard.

Helpful hint: When using tempera paint, mix with a small amount of Staflo starch. This makes the paint adhere to the paper better, so you won't experience flaking, plus it gives a nice sheen to the finish. In addition, you can make fingerpaint by using a 50-50 mixture of tempera paint and starch. By so doing, your material costs will be substantially reduced.

Occasionally, you may need to obtain special items—pipe cleaners, clothespins, Popsicle sticks, wiggly eyes, elastic string, small magnets, needlepoint netting. Some of the projects call for "tacky glue." This refers to a product such as Dennison's Tack-a-Note, a glue stick with a special adhesive for temporarily fastening bits of paper to displays, but which allows for removal and replacement elsewhere.

Whenever possible, we recommend the use of recycled materials—items such as wallpaper samples, round pizza cardboard, empty cans and plastic containers, used foam carpet padding, fake fur and fabric scraps, used boxes and bags, and cardboard scraps. This keeps projects inexpensive and earth-friendly, too.

Where Do You Go From Here?

If you enjoy *BodyArt: People,* you may also be interested in the two other books with this creative approach to learning. *BodyArt: Holidays* covers birthdays, Halloween, harvest time, Christmas, Hannukah, Valentine's Day, and Groundhog Day. *BodyArt: Nature* features four-legged animals, birds, fish, insects, spiders, and seasons.

What is BodyArt?

Like all activities that build self-esteem, BodyArt begins with the children. The projects are based on hands, fingers, feet, toes, and other body parts. These basic shapes are enhanced with a wide variety of free or inexpensive art materials.

Colors are bright and brash, lines are big and bold, shapes are repeated over and over again. The whole process of creating is a magical world for the child, bursting with excitement and unique, meaningful involvement.

Intricately woven into children's artwork is their imagination, their personal perception of what they see or make. When faced with a circle, adults see a circle; but a child who has just drawn a circle may see a hot air balloon, an iridescent bubble, or a turtle with its head and feet pulled in. BodyArt draws on a young child's imagination and creativity.

Each child makes a unique contribution to a BodyArt project. It's much more than coloring in the lines or filling in a worksheet. Without the child's hand, head, fingers, toes, feet, or body, there is no artwork. As a result, the final product can be treasured for years as a tribute to the child's talents and growth.

The projects themselves are fun and easy to do. There's involvement for children of every age. At the earliest developmental level, children will simply provide the necessary body part for tracing and cutting by the adult; they'll then decorate the shape. More advanced children can trace the shapes and assist in the cutting. Older children will be able to handle all the tasks. However much the young artists do, their efforts will lead to increased confidence. Each "I did it" experience prepares children for motivation and achievement at ever-higher levels of learning.

Think of BodyArt as being a branch of the "whole language" tree of learning. BodyArt is a limb that reaches out to the healthy, egocentric needs of young children in the following ways:

- BodyArt uses language for real, meaningful purposes so that children are able to make sense of their world and their place in it.
- BodyArt actively involves children through experiential, inductive, and democratic processes.
- BodyArt recognizes the learning environment as a social community where educational resources are found.
- BodyArt incorporates a wide variety of tactile, kinesthetic, visual, and listening activities that reach all learning styles.
- BodyArt is highly adaptable to the typical learner, as well as to gifted and talented and to learning disabled children.

Enjoy the units and prepare for wonderful days ahead with these BodyArt activities.

Worries and Fears

Things that go bump in the night, a dog that's sick, a lost cat or jacket—these are the sorts of worries and fears children often have. By bringing such concerns out in the open, we can make them smaller and more manageable for the child. Children who have vivid imaginations are especially prone to worry. For example, when their mom and dad disagree, children may be upset with themselves because of the perceived part they imagine they had in the parents' argument. All the buried imaginings of the day may come to the forefront at night, in the dark. Bad dreams can confuse and haunt young children, especially because they can't distinguish between dreams and reality. Adults can help children cope with their fears and master their uneasy feelings.

"Feelings" Bulletin Board

It's often easy to read children's feelings on their faces. That's the idea behind this "Here's What I'm Feeling Today" bulletin board. This activity helps children learn to name their feelings and recognize them.

Trace each child's head and hair on a piece of white paper. Decorate the paper heads with only hair, nose, and ears, gluing patches of Velcro in the position of eyes and mouth. Post on the bulletin board, identifying each head with the child's name. Then on separate sheets, have children draw happy eyes and mouths, sad eyes and mouths, and worried eyes and mouths.

Each day the children choose the appropriate eyes and mouth to match how they are feeling. To provide a nonthreatening atmosphere, explain that it's okay if someone chooses not to participate. Perhaps on another day the child may want to join in, or may seek you out privately to discuss particular worries, fears, or bad dreams.

My Very Own Monster

Materials: construction paper, crayons, white paper.

Sometimes adults tend to discount a child's fear of monsters hiding in the closet, saying, "There are no monsters in there." This project instead helps the children visually describe the monsters that bother them most. In this way the children can face their fear and rid their closets of anything but clothes.

Trace each child's foot and one or two hands on a sheet of white paper. Cut out and glue to construction paper. There is no "correct" way to position the paper hand and foot. It all depends on how the children envision their very own scary monsters! The children add details with crayons.

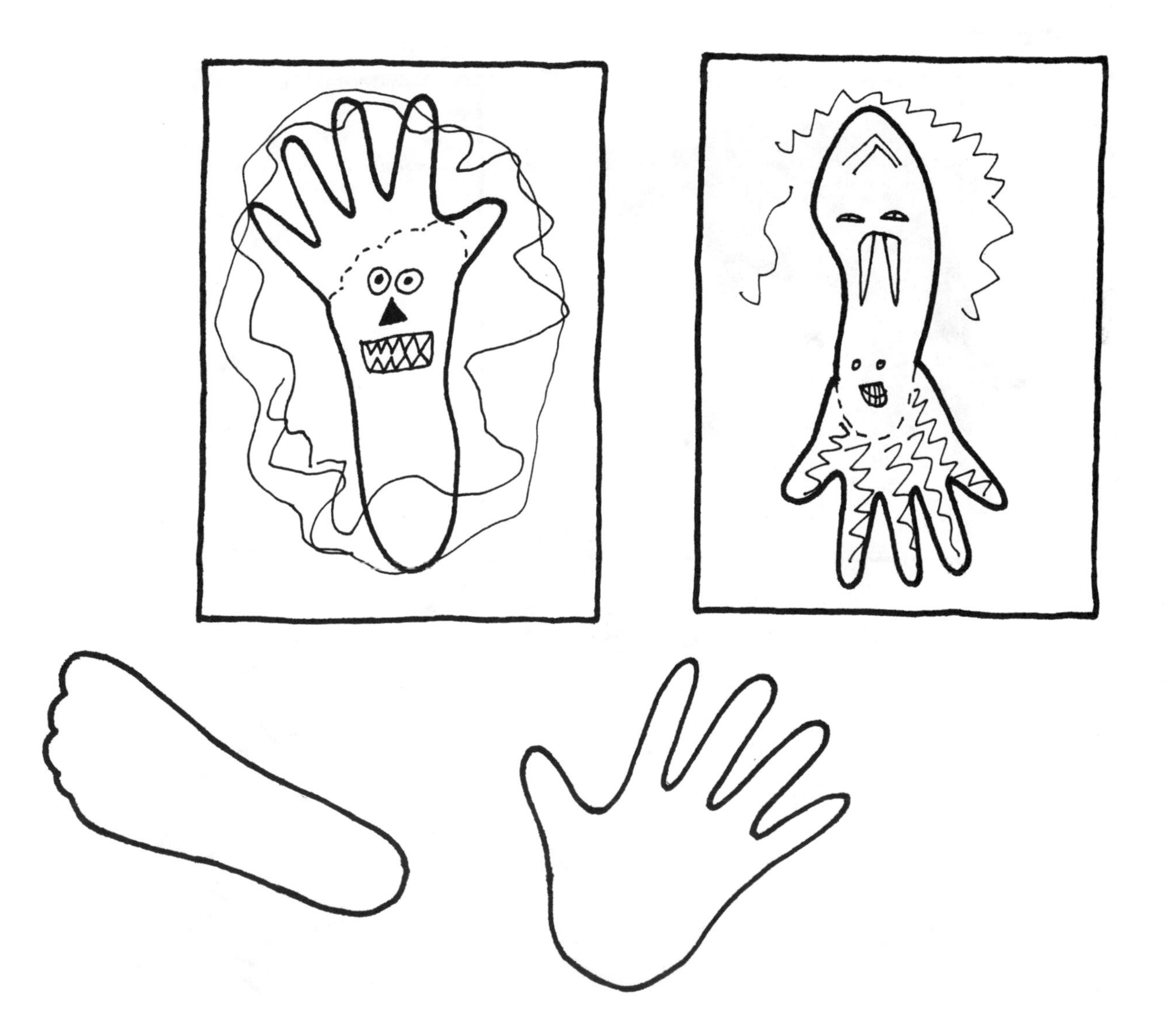

Night-Mare

Materials: construction paper, nontoxic paint, yarn, glue.

With a little play on words, a scary "nightmare" turns into a small, not-so-scary—and even protective—horse. (See "The Nightmare Poem" later in this chapter.)

To make each night-mare (horse, that is!), dip the child's hand in tempera and make a handprint on the paper. The thumb represents the horse's head, so extend it as far as possible. After the print dries, glue on scraps of yarn to make a mane and tail.

Rainbow Kids Hands

Materials: white construction paper, tongue depressors, nontoxic fingerpaints in red, orange, yellow, green, blue, purple.

Rainbows are bright and happy images—a perfect way to congratulate young children for doing battle with the scary things that bother them. Call your group "the Rainbow Kids" as they create these cheerful hands, which can be used with the "We're Not Afraid of Anything" movement song in this chapter.

Put a narrow strip of each color of fingerpaint into a flat container. Then have each child dip one hand gently into the paint and press it onto construction paper to create a rainbow hand. Glue each hand onto a tongue depressor when dry.

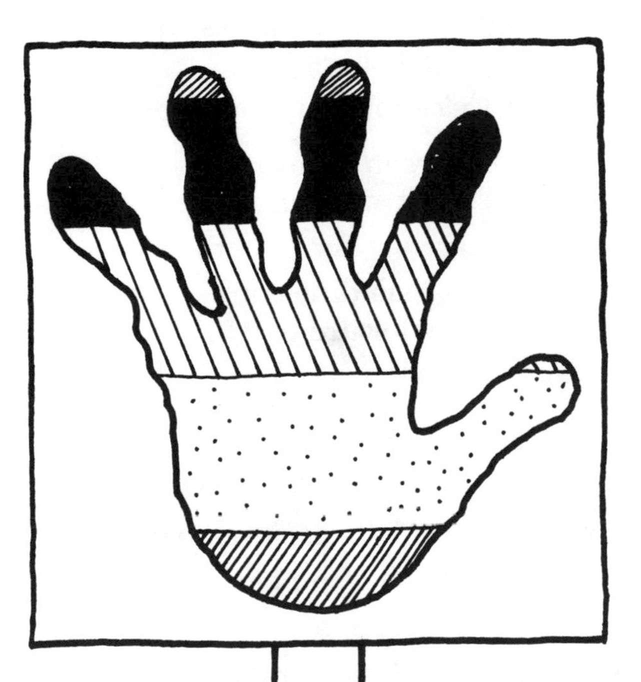

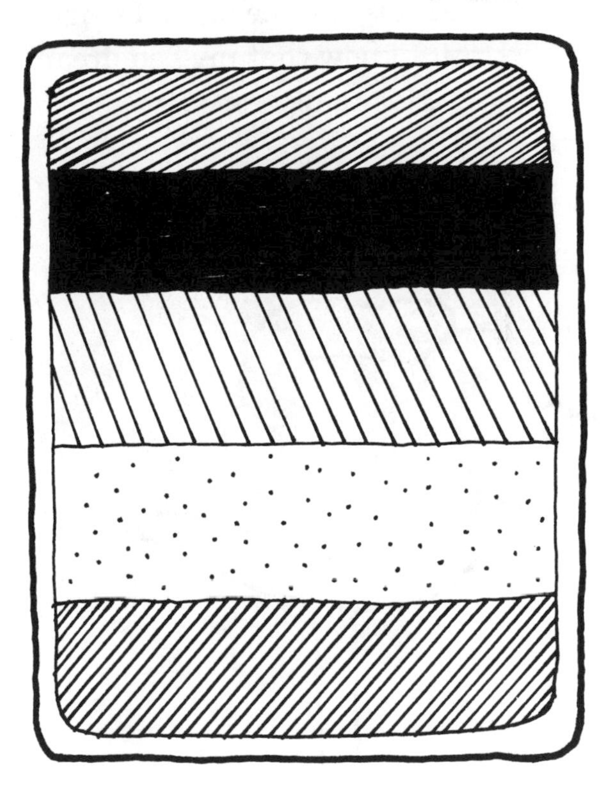

Worries and Fears Poem and Movement Songs

The Nightmare Poem

There's a nightmare in my closet.
She's as dark as dark can be,
And when she rears
her handsome head
Her neighs are full of glee.

There's nothing bad about her.
She's kind and full of fun.
And when I have a bad dream,
She'll come out on the run.

She'll stamp her feet,
And swish her tail,
She'll toss her head, and neigh,
Until I know that my bad dream
Has really gone away.

We're Not Afraid of Anything!

(Sung to "Mary Had a Little Lamb")

We're not afraid of anything,
anything, anything,
we're not afraid of anything
'cause we're the Rainbow Kids!

Lions and tigers don't scare us,
don't scare us, don't scare us,
lions and tigers don't scare us,
'cause we're the Rainbow Kids!

Monsters and snakes
don't scare us,
don't scare us, don't scare us,
monsters and snakes
don't scare us,
'cause we're the Rainbow Kids!

Big, green dinosaurs
don't scare us,
don't scare us, don't scare us,
big, green dinosaurs
don't scare us,
'cause we're the Rainbow Kids!

Vampires and bats don't scare us,
don't scare us, don't scare us,
vampires and bats don't scare us,
'cause we're the Rainbow Kids!

Teacher note: Pictures of the scary things mentioned can be attached to tongue depressors and held up whenever the scary thing is named in the song. With the last line of each verse, the children can hold up and wave their Rainbow Kids hands.

Worries and Fears Read-Alouds

Fiction Picture Books

Aylesworth, Jim. *Two Terrible Frights.* New York: Atheneum, 1987.

The little mouse in the basement and the little girl upstairs have two things in common. They both want a bedtime snack, and they both have a terrible fright when they see each other!

Browne, Anthony. *Willy the Wimp.* New York: Alfred A. Knopf, 1984.

Everybody bullies Willy until he sends away for a body building book and learns how to defend himself. In the process, Willy learns that how he feels about himself directly affects how people feel about him.

Gackenbach, Dick. *Harry and the Terrible Whatzit.* New York: Clarion Books, 1977.

Harry overcomes his fear of the Terrible Whatzit in order to save his mother.

Giff, Patricia Reilly. *Today Was a Terrible Day.* New York: Puffin Books, 1980.

Ronald Morgan has a terrible day at school. His friends nickname him Snakey. He signs his mother's name on his homework and gets caught. And, he eats another boy's salami sandwich. Luckily, with Miss Tyler's help, Ronald's day is not completely ruined.

Hazbry, Nancy and Roy Condy. *How to Get Rid of Bad Dreams.* New York: Scholastic, 1983.

Here's a bunch of ideas for making bad dreams and scary monsters go away—show them a mirror of themselves; pull out your shrink-ray laser; take out a can of silver paint and spray it on them. In short: laugh right back at them!

Kent, Jack. *There's No Such Thing as a Dragon.* New York: Golden Books, 1975.

Billy Bixbee and his mom learn that fears don't go away when you ignore them.

Kherdian, David and Nonny Hogrogrian. *Right Now.* New York: Alfred A. Knopf, 1983.

Life is full of ups and downs. Yesterday a lost cat, a fall from a bike, a new teacher, but right now it's just fine—with mud cookies and a run through a meadow.

Stinson, Kathy. *Those Green Things.* Toronto: Annick Press, 1985.

A little girl's vivid imagination turns green socks in the laundry basket into lizards eating her T-shirts, and green pajamas under the bed into giant frogs.

Viorst, Judith. *Alexander and the Terrible, Horrible, No Good, Very Bad Day.* New York: Macmillan, 1987.

Talk about getting up on the wrong side of the bed! Alexander starts the day by tripping on his skateboard and dropping his sweater in the sink while the water is running.

Viorst, Judith. *My Mama Says There Aren't Any Zombies, Ghosts, Vampires, Creatures, Demons, Monsters, Fiends, Goblins, or Things.* New York: Macmillan, 1987.

How can a boy believe his mom about the big things—zombies, ghosts, vampires—when she's mistaken about the little things, like the location of the cream cheese in the refrigerator?

Worries and Fears Snacktime

Monster Juice

You may be tempted to add food coloring to milk to create a monster's strange brew, but children will turn up their noses at an altered snack that looks different but tastes the same. Here's a "monster juice" that they'll happily consume. In a blender combine 1/2 cup plain low-fat yogurt, 1 egg, 1 teaspoon sugar, and 2 cups mashed bananas. Blend on high until smooth. Chill or serve over ice. Serves 2-3 little monsters; adjust quantities according to the number in your group.

Worries and Fears Game

Monster Movement

Materials: light source, black construction paper, white crayon. Optional: white construction paper, nontoxic paints, crayons or markers in a variety of colors.

Use a projector or another light source (such as a flashlight or lamp) to project a shadow of a child's hands on the wall. Encourage the children to arrange fingers to create their own hand monsters. Depending on the distance the hands are held from the light, the monster shape will be either large or small. After exploring possible monster shapes and sizes, trace one of the child's shadows onto black construction paper. If desired, use white paper so that monsters can be painted or colored with crayons or markers.

Feelings on My Face

In this activity, you can help children identify different feelings associated with common worries and fears. Hand out copies of the Feelings on My Face reproducible (see next page). Read aloud each word on the left and talk about times someone might feel that way. After discussing each word, the children can draw an expression on the face to the right. Being able to name an unhappy feeling is part of learning to conquer a particular worry or fear.

Often, the choice of dark colors or scribbling will be how a child represents these dark feelings. For example, a child who has recently experienced a fire or another personal crisis at home might color the picture totally black, with no facial details. This is a perfectly good response to the activity, and indicates a healthy ability to express worries and fears.

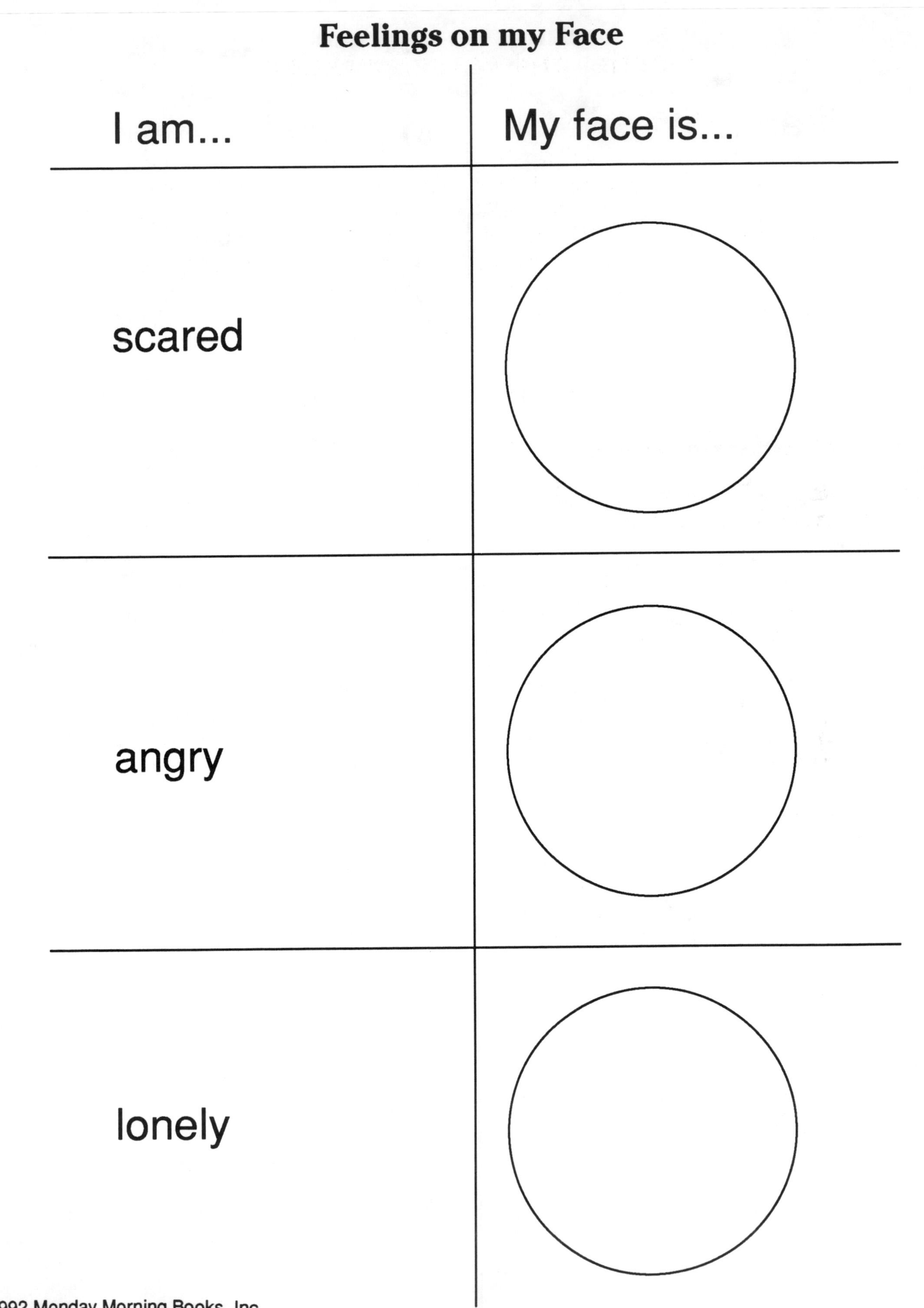
Feelings on my Face
I am...
My face is...
scared
angry
lonely

Feelings on my Face

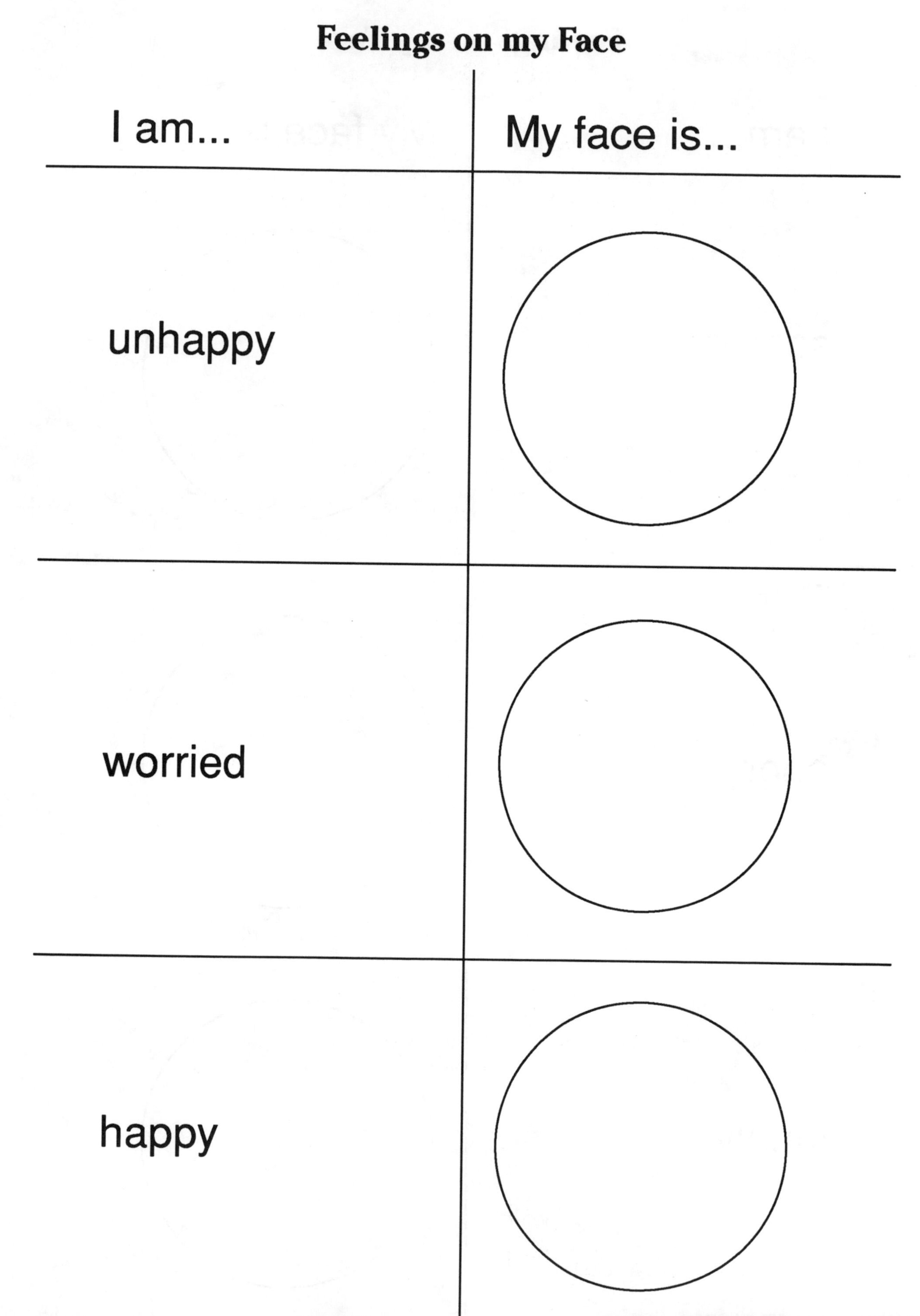

Feeling Fine

A child's early years are important for development of self-esteem. As children master physical coordination, cognitive skills, and awareness of feelings, they gain self-confidence. As a result, a healthy egocentricity evolves through nurturing the child's positive self-esteem.

BodyArt projects affirm a child's unique self-concept. The activities in "Feeling Fine" give children an opportunity to feel pride in their own special abilities while at the same time learning to be sensitive to other children's abilities and feelings.

"Oh You Beautiful Baby" Bulletin Board

Children change so quickly in their early years, it's fun to share those changes with one another.

To make your bulletin board, have the children bring in their own baby pictures. You will also need current photos, which you can snap yourself or have the children bring from home.

Attach several long strips of Velcro (soft side) horizontally across your bulletin board. Then attach a small square of Velcro (loop side) to the back top center of each picture.

See the Guessing Game later in this chapter for a way to make this an interactive bulletin board.

Teacher note: Pressure sensitive Velcro works well, and there's no chance of damaging photos as could happen with glue or tape.

Hand Plaque

Materials: plaster of Paris, plastic mixing bowl, measuring cup, water, plastic spatula, food coloring, disposable plastic plates (recycled microwave meal trays make wonderful forms). Optional: tempera paint, paper clips.

This BodyArt project will result in a permanent handprint that parents and children can cherish for years to come.

Mix up a batch of plaster of Paris according to package directions. Pour mixture into individual plastic dishes. Allow each child to personalize with color by squirting a small amount of food coloring into his or her dish. Stir with a Popsicle stick to create an interesting pattern.

When plaster of Paris becomes firm enough to make an impression (about 10-15 minutes), press the child's hand gently into it. Allow plaque to dry (about 45 minutes). Then remove by gently flexing the sides of the dish.

After the plaque is dry, you can make the hand stand out by dipping the child's hand in tempera paint (any color) and making a print inside the existing impression.

Teacher note: To make a hanging plaque, use a bent paper clip. Hold the long tip of the paper clip over one side of the dish. Then pour on plaster of Paris mixture, making sure to cover all the remaining paper clip. Position child's hand so that the paper clip is at the top of the dish.

Don't be hesitant to use plaster of Paris. Just remember to use plastic utensils and containers. After plaster hardens, the remains simply break away and fall off, so clean up is easy. Never, under any circumstances, pour plaster of Paris mixture (even if diluted) down the drain. It will solidify in your pipes.

“I Like Me” Body Tracing

Materials: long rolls of white paper (end rolls of printing paper) or brown butcher paper, crayons, nontoxic washable markers, tape.

Children love to make life-sized reproductions of themselves. To make a body tracing, first allow the children their choice of floor or wall so that they won’t feel insecure. Sometimes lying down on the floor is very threatening for a young child.

Tape paper to wall or floor and have each child either stand against or lie on the paper. You will then use markers to trace the child’s entire body. The children can draw in hair and facial features and color in the clothes they are wearing that day to make a paper replica of themselves.

Growing Hand

Materials: clean Styrofoam meat tray (recycled), grass seed, nontoxic glue, black permanent marker, potting soil, water, plastic wrap.

In this three-dimensional project, the children see their hands "grow"!

Trace a child's hand with marker on a Styrofoam tray. Fill in hand outline with glue. Then pour grass seed over hand and shake off excess. Fill meat tray with potting soil. Wrap loosely with plastic wrap to help keep moisture in so that soil does not dry out. Then place trays in a sunny spot and water daily. In a very short period of time, the hand will begin to grow out of the meat tray.

Teacher note: If desired, use beans and other seeds instead of grass seed to fill in the hand. However, do not cover with potting soil; leave the seeds exposed. This makes a nice keepsake for the child to take home.

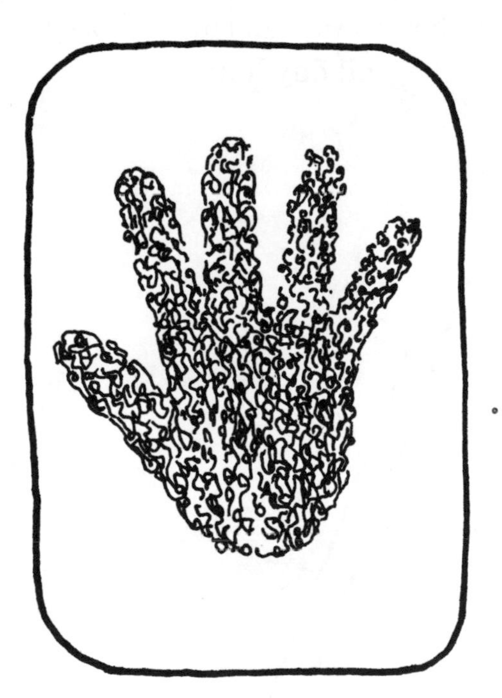

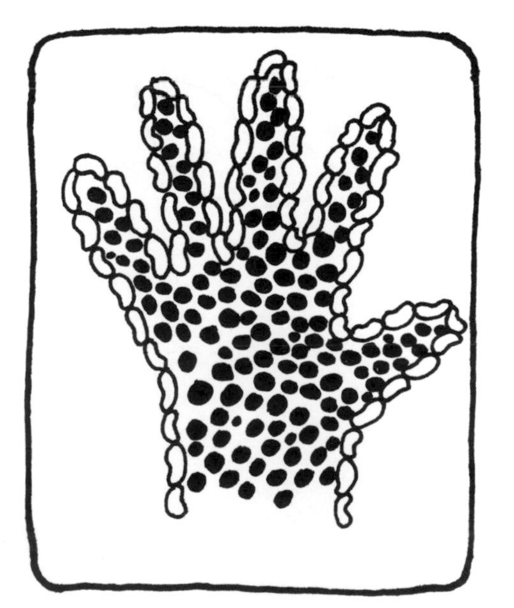

Feeling Fine Rhymes and Movement Songs

Feeling Fine

Let me tell you all I can do—
Touch my toes and count to two.
Brush my teeth and put on a shoe.
Wiggle my nose and climb a tree.
That's what I can do at three!

When I'm four there's so much more—
Help my mom and open the door.
Throw a ball and sweep the floor.
Draw a circle, draw a line.
I'm so great, I'm feeling fine!

Teacher note: Children do (or pantomime) each of the actions mentioned as they chant the rhyme.

My Body

(Sung to "London Bridge")

Watch my body twist this way,
twist this way, twist this way,
Watch my body twist this way,
all day long.

Watch my two arms stretch this way,
stretch this way, stretch this way,
Watch my two arms stretch this way,
all day long.

Watch my two legs run this way,
run this way, run this way,
Watch my two legs run this way,
all day long.

Wonder Child

(Sung to "London Bridge")

I am such a wonder child,
wonder child, wonder child,
I am such a wonder child.
Yes, I really am!

I can dance and play and run,
play and run, play and run,
I can dance and play and run.
Yes, I really can!

I can color, draw and paint,
draw and paint, draw and paint,
I can color, draw and paint,
Yes, I really can!

I can talk and sing and shout,
sing and shout, sing and shout,
I can talk and sing and shout.
Yes, I really can!

Bedtime Song

(Sung to "Mulberry Bush")

What do we do when it's time for bed,
Time for bed, time for bed?
What do we do when it's time for bed?
We go and brush our teeth.

We brush and brush and brush our teeth,
Brush our teeth, brush our teeth.
We brush and brush and brush our teeth,
Before we go to bed.

Teacher note: This song is a nice accompaniment to *The Bed Book* by Sylvia Plath. Make up additional verses based on appropriate pre-bedtime or pre-naptime activities. For example: put on our pajamas, go and find our blanket, sit and read a book, give mom a hug and kiss.

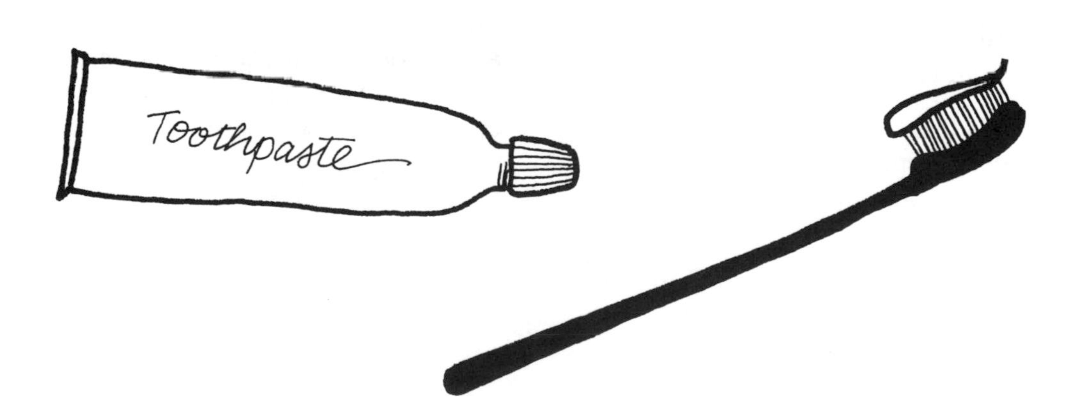

Feeling Fine Read-Alouds

Fiction Picture Books

Baynton, Martin. *Jane and the Dragon.* Martinez, CA: Discovery Toys, 1988.

Jane wants to be a knight in shining armor, which is unheard of for a woman in the Middle Ages, but she courageously meets the challenges required of any brave knight.

Brown, Marc. *Arthur's Eyes.* Boston: Atlantic Monthly Press, 1977.

Arthur's friends laugh at him when he wears his new glasses. He decides not to wear them but finds out a person can get into big trouble that way. Gradually, Arthur accepts his glasses—and so do his friends.

Brown, Marc. *Arthur's Nose.* New York: Trumpet Club, 1976.

Arthur decides to go to a rhinologist to get a new nose. He doesn't like his old nose, but the ones suggested by the doctor don't look right either. They just aren't, well . . . Arthur!

Carlson, Nancy. *I Like Me.* New York: Puffin Books, 1990.

The self-confident heroine of this story is a girl pig who likes everything about herself—from her curly tail and round tummy to her tiny little feet. This wonderful picture book is bound to help children find reasons to like themselves.

Geringer, Laura. *A Three Hat Day.* New York: Harper & Row, 1985.

Hats open a magical door to self-awareness. Read all about R.R. Pottle's hats, then let the children play dress-up with hats you have collected.

Heathers, Anne and Estebam Frances. *A Handful of Surprises.* New York: Harcourt, Brace & World, 1961.

Fleek the clown and his glove puppets are mischief makers who don't always agree, but huddle for mutual comfort from time to time.

Muhtean, Michaela. *The Little Engine That Could and The Big Chase.* New York: Platt & Munk, 1988.

For many years the little blue engine has helped children learn the value of overcoming fears to try a difficult task. It's still a self-esteem booster today.

Plath, Sylvia. *The Bed Book.* New York: Harper & Row, 1976.

Ordinary beds are replaced by wonderfully imaginative ones in this whimsical look at bedtime.

Parnall, Peter. *Feet!* New York: Macmillan, 1988.

All kinds of feet are described in this humorous offering that also helps children learn the richness of language.

Wood, Audrey. *Quick as a Cricket.* Singapore: Child's Play, 1982.

This great self-esteem book helps children accept everything about themselves. A side benefit: learning common metaphors!

Zolotow, Charlotte. *I Like to Be Little.* New York: Harper & Row, 1987.

Many children can't wait to grow up and do adult things (like stay up late at night). In this story there's so many reasons why a girl likes being a child, it makes parents wish they were children again. Best of all, this book makes children aware of all the good things that go along with childhood—a once in a lifetime experience!

Nonfiction

Aliki. *Feelings.* New York: Greenwillow, 1984.

This delightful book covers the full range of emotions and helps children recognize and accept their own feelings. Featured on PBS "Reading Rainbow."

Aliki. *My Hands.* New York: Thomas Y. Crowell, 1962.

Finger facts are described in this charming "Let's Read and Find-Out" science book.

Cole, Joanna. *The Magic School Bus Inside the Human Body.* New York: Scholastic, 1989.

Interesting look at what's inside the human body with child-appropriate illustrations.

Ruis, Maria. *The Five Senses: Smell.* New York: Barron's, 1985.

Excellent nonfiction picture book series that explains the senses to even the youngest preschooler. Other titles explore sight, hearing, taste, and touch.

Sullivan, Mary Beth and Linda Bourke. *A Show of Hands: Say It in Sign Language.* New York: Addison-Wesley, 1980.

Some 14 million people are deaf or hearing impaired. With this book, older preschoolers can learn the sign language for *sad, silly,* and a whole range of feelings. Featured on PBS "Reading Rainbow."

Feeling Fine Snacktime

Handful of Cookies

The easiest way to make this delicious snack is to buy prepared sugar cookie dough from the refrigerated section of your local food store. Roll out this dough. Trace child's hand with a butter knife. Remove excess dough from around the dough hand, and use a spatula to carefully transfer to a cookie sheet.

If desired, use toothpicks to carefully write the child's name on the dough hand before baking. Then bake according to package directions.

Teacher note: Since the children will be eating their hand cookies, be sure to have their real hands washed before the tracing.

Feeling Fine Game

Guessing Game

Use your "Oh You Beautiful Baby" bulletin board as a basis for this simple guessing game. Children will take turns guessing which baby picture belongs to which child's picture. In order to play this game, encourage secrecy when the children first bring their baby pictures to school, but any child who wants to proudly share his or her picture immediately should be allowed to do so.

My Body Puzzle

Make copies of the My Body Puzzle pages for each child. Color and cut apart the pieces. (The puzzles can be copied on paper of various colors for different skin tones.) Use the My Body Puzzle for practice in naming parts of the body as well as finding how the parts fit together.

My Body Puzzle

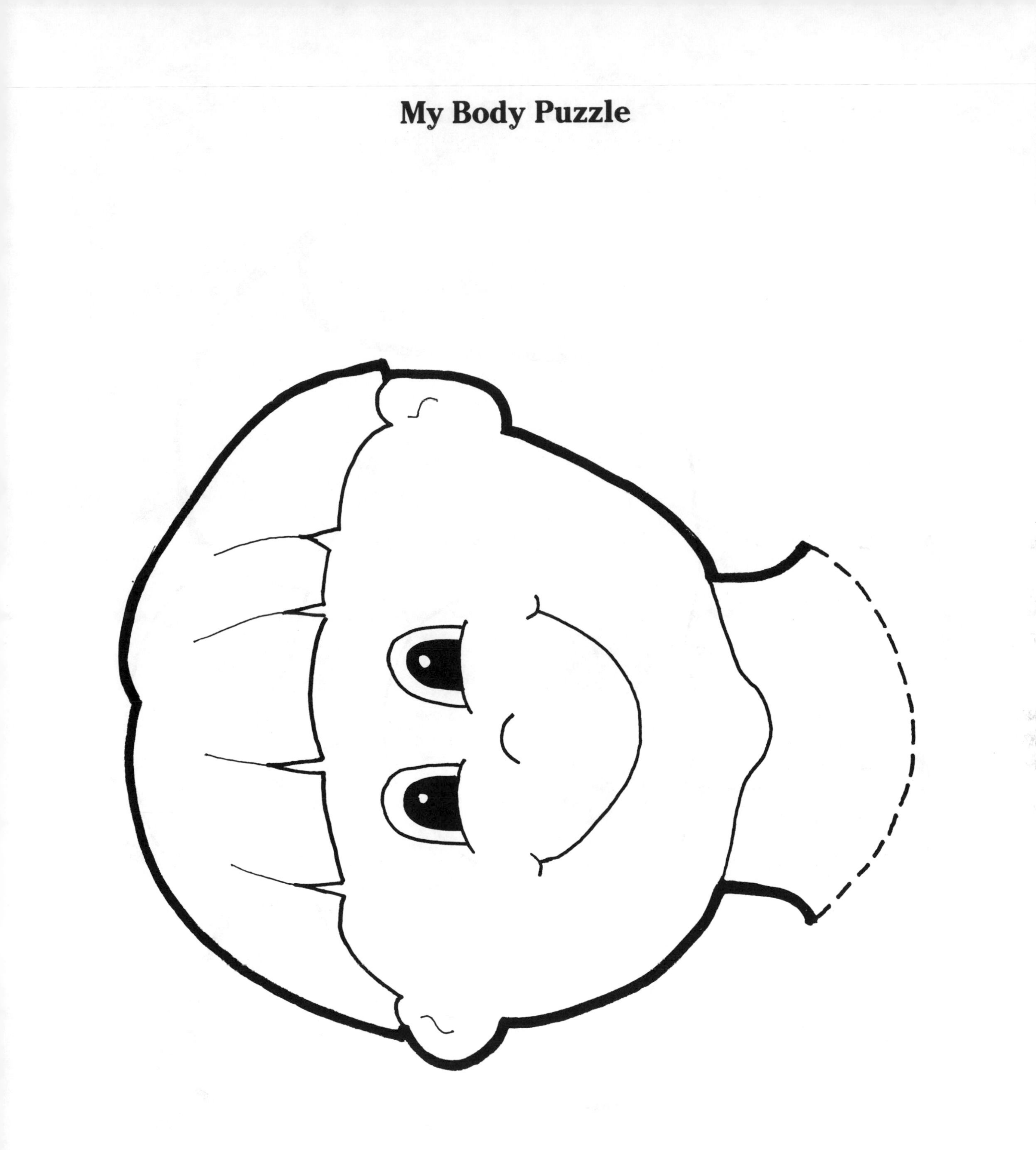

My Body Puzzle

My Body Puzzle

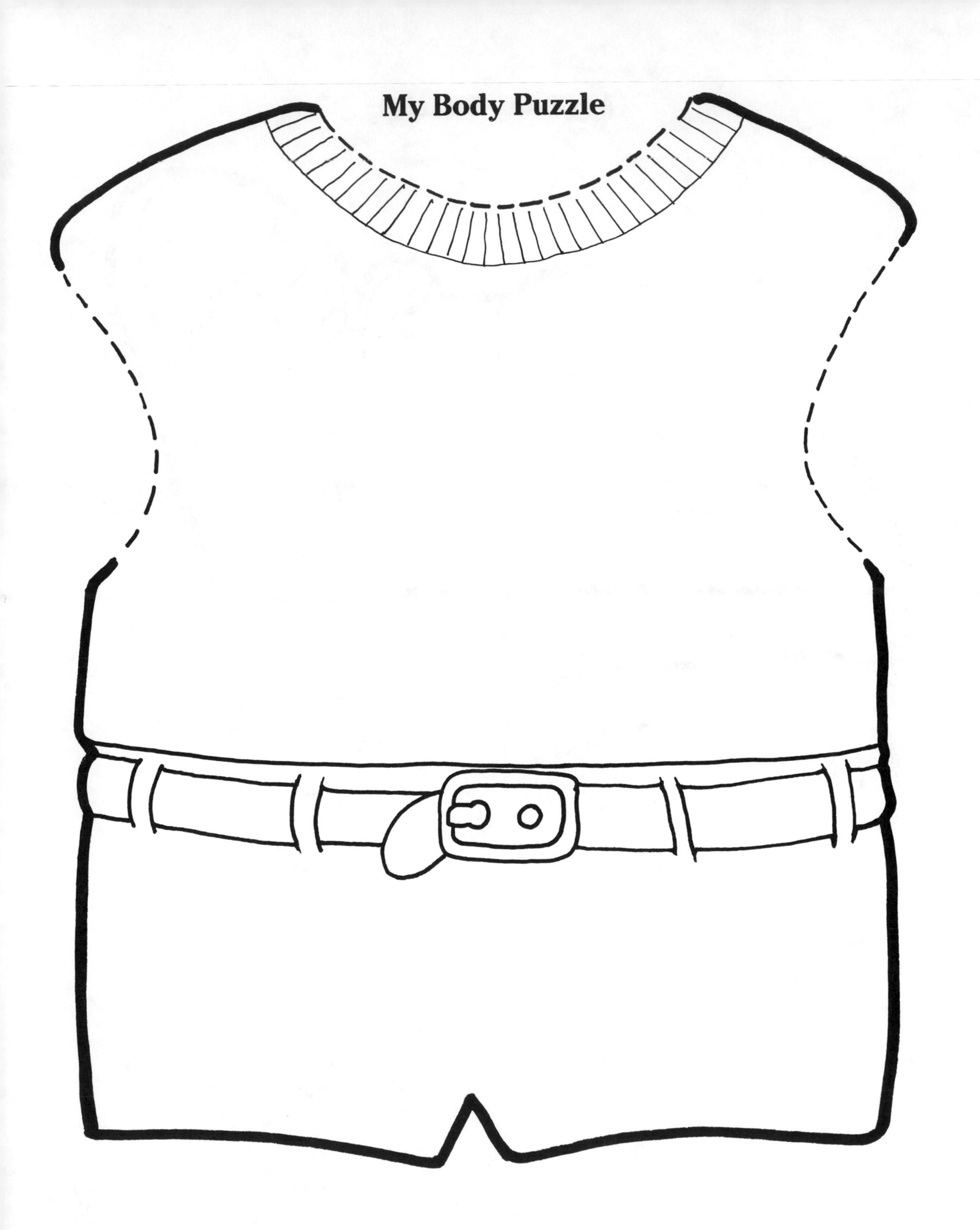

My Body Puzzle

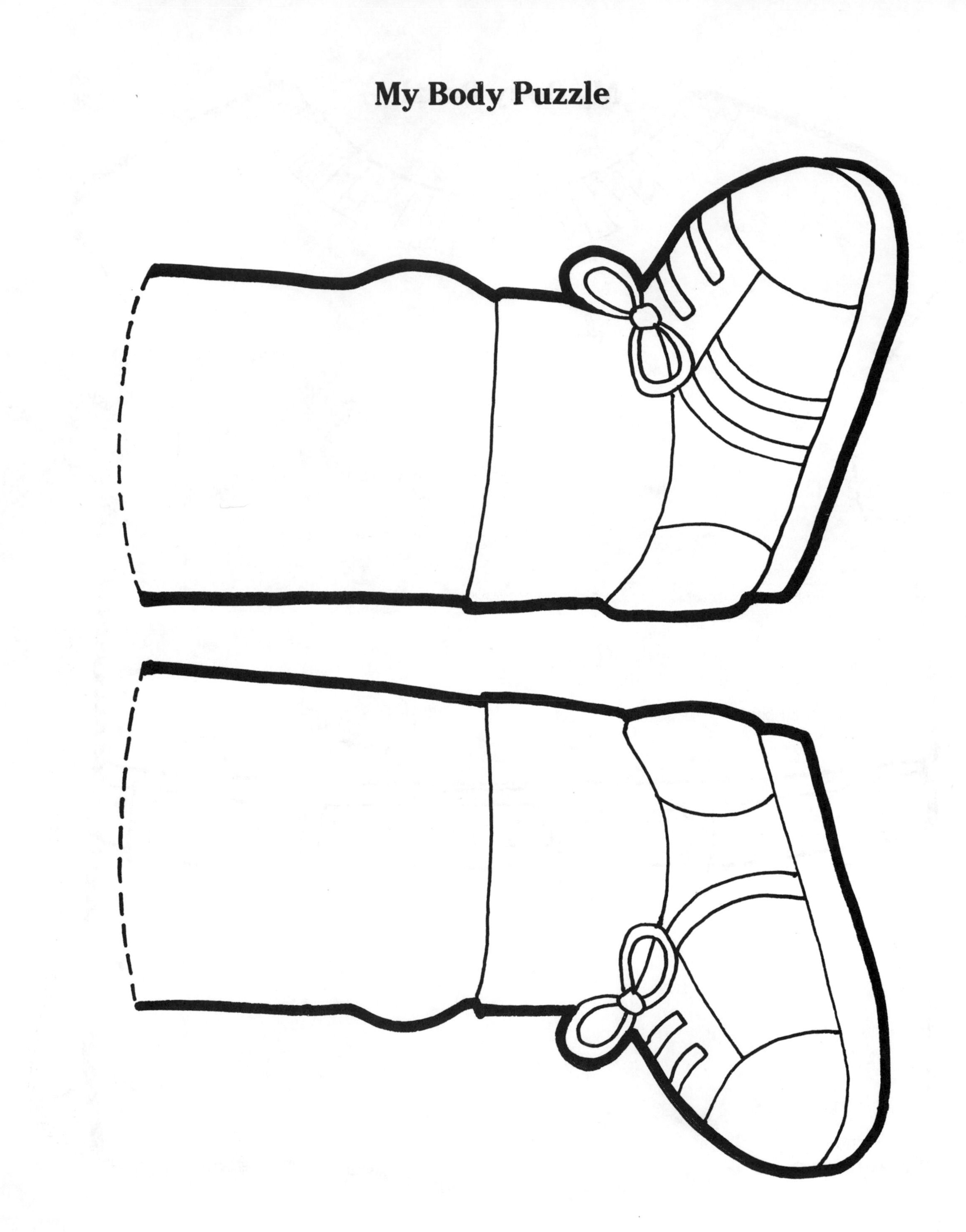

My Body Puzzle

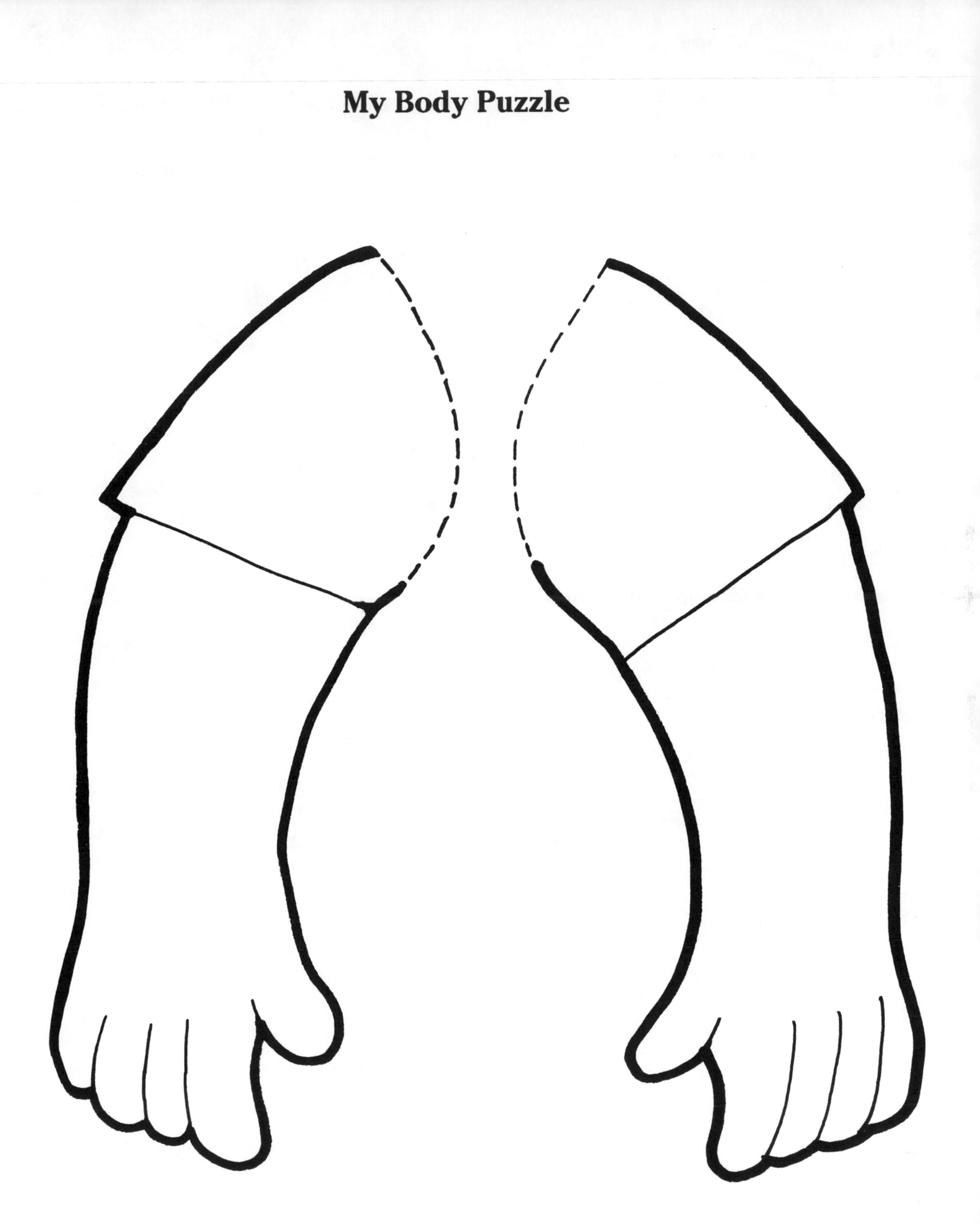

Fabulous Families

Even before the child gains self-awareness, familial bonding takes place. Studies have indicated this bonding occurs even before the actual birth of the child. Bonding to the family—whether traditional or nontraditional—needs to be nurtured in order for children to grow physically, cognitively, and emotionally. Through positive nurturing, children are able to grow and expand their boundaries to include extended family structures—grandparents, aunts, uncles, stepmoms, stepdads, and so forth.

Fabulous Families BodyArt projects are designed to enhance the children's awareness of their position within the family. Through this awareness they will be able to expand their positive self-concept while building a foundation for later friendships.

"Family Trees are Special" Bulletin Board

To celebrate each family's special uniqueness, ask parents to provide a family snapshot for a "Family Trees" bulletin board display. Trace a teacher-size hand and arm on brown paper to make a large tree trunk and branches. Glue in the center of a large sheet of bulletin board paper. Attach the children's family photos to the branches of the tree to represent leaves. Some children may have more than one photo if they are part of more than one family.

A single tree will work for a group of six or seven children. Create as many trees as needed for the entire class. Discuss with the group the differences in individual families. Use this as a time to assure children that no matter who makes up their family structure, it is still a family—very special and not lacking in any way.

Coat of Arms

Materials: copies of the reproducible shield (see end of this chapter), scissors, nontoxic tempera paint, nontoxic washable markers or crayons. Optional: safety pins, tagboard.

The coat of arms (also known as a family crest) is a visual symbol of the idea that each family is unique and special. For each coat of arms, make a copy of the shield. You may want to transfer it to tagboard for durability.

Print the child's name in the top section of the shield. Children can then color or decorate the shield and cut out. Dip each child's hand into tempera paint and press onto the bottom section.

Teacher note: If desired, safety pins can be used to attach the coat of arms to a child's clothing to wear proudly throughout the day.

My Own Family Tree

Materials: 11 x 14 inch construction paper, 8 1/2 x 11 inch construction paper (variety of colors), crayons, nontoxic glue, scissors.

Just like children, no two families are alike. Thus each child's family tree will be different from all the others.

Trace each child's hand (fingers open) and arm onto the large construction paper to represent tree trunk and branches. Children can then color in the outline.

To make leaves, trace each child's hand (fingers open) on smaller sheets of construction paper and cut out. Repeat as many times as needed. Have the child draw a picture of one family member on each hand leaf.

If desired, you can print the names with the child's pictures—mom, dad, grandma, grandpa, and so on. Glue onto tree branches.

Walking Shoes

Materials: cardboard, scissors, crayons, thick rubber bands, another family member's shoes (flats only).

Give your children an opportunity to walk in someone else's shoes and introduce or reinforce left and right discrimination to boot! The shoes that each child brings from home should belong to an adult, or at least someone bigger than the child.

Trace on cardboard each pair of shoes brought from home. Cut out and attach to the children's own shoes with rubber bands.

Have fun marching around the room to the "Walking Shoes March" provided in this chapter.

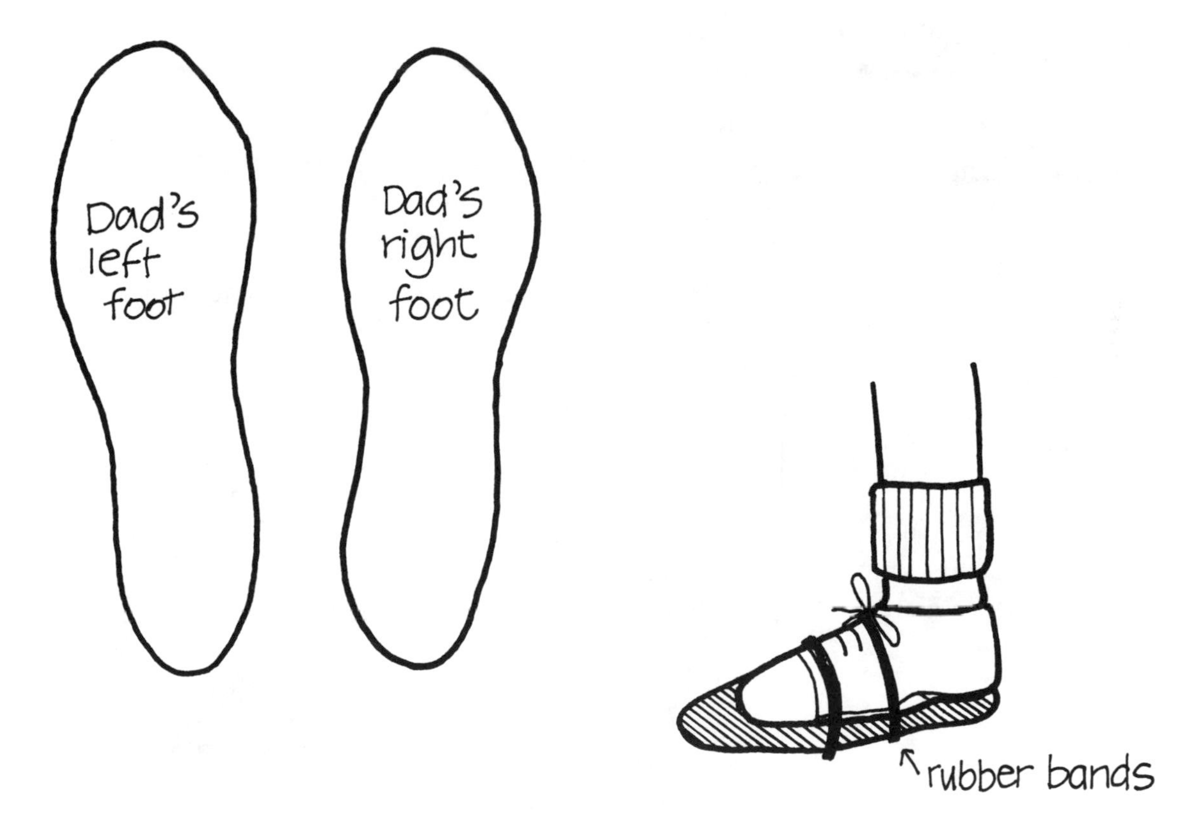

Families Movement Song

Walking Shoes March

Left, right, left, right
I'm walking in somebody's shoes.
Are they your mommy's shoes?
(Children answer either "Mine are!" or "Not mine!")
Are they your daddy's shoes?
(Mine are!/Not mine!)
Are they your uncle's shoes?
(Mine are!/Not mine!)
Are they your granny's shoes?
(Mine are!/Not mine!)
Are they your brother's shoes?
(Mine are!/Not mine!)
Left, right, left, right,
I'm walking in somebody's shoes.

Teacher note: This marching chant is to be used with the BodyArt Walking Shoes project. As the children march around the room with the oversize shoes on their feet, they individually answer each of the questions in the chant with either "Mine are!" or "Not mine!" according to whose shoes they are wearing. Add questions as necessary to cover all the possibilities in your group.

Families Read-Alouds

Fiction Picture Books

Aliki. *Jack and Jake.* New York: Greenwillow Books, 1986.

Jack and Jake are identical twins, and even their family finds it hard to tell them apart. This is especially nice for those twins in your group.

Barrett, Judy. *Cloudy with a Chance of Meatballs.* New York: Macmillan, 1978.

Grandpas tell the neatest stories! This one starts with a mis-flipped pancake and turns into an adventure-packed story about the tiny town of Chewandswallow.

Berenstain, Stan and Jan. *The Berenstain Bears and the Week at Grandma's.* New York: Random House, 1986.

When mama and papa go on their second honeymoon, brother and sister bear go to grandma's and grandpa's house.

Boyd, Lizi. *The Not-So-Wicked Stepmother.* New York: Puffin Books, 1989.

Hessie knows all about wicked, mean, and ugly stepmothers, but she's not prepared for this nice one!

Brown, Marcia and Charles Perrault. *Cinderella and the Little Glass Slipper.* New York: Charles Scribner's Sons, 1954.

This Caldecott Medal version of the familiar fairy tale is also an example of a blended family gone awry.

Browne, Anthony. *Piggyback.* New York: Alfred A. Knopf, 1986.

The Piggott's find out what happens when they take mother for granted and she leaves them with the mess they made.

Clifton, Lucille. *Everett Anderson's Goodbye.* New York: Trumpet, 1983.

Everett goes through the five stages of grief in this sensitive book that tells about the loss of a dad. Featured on PBS "Reading Rainbow."

Cole, Babette. *The Trouble with Dad.* New York: G.P. Putnam's Sons, 1985.

Robots are the trouble with dad. He likes to make them—all kinds. Why? Because he has a boring job. Fortunately, the robots are very valuable to the person who buys them all and makes dad very rich.

Gauch, Patricia Lee. *Christina Katerina and the Time She Quit the Family.* New York: G.P. Putnam's Sons, 1987.

On a perfectly good Saturday at quarter past nine, Christina Katerina quits the family. She even changes her name to Agnes and divides up the house!

Greenfield, Eloise. *Grandpa's Face.* New York: Philomel, 1991.

When grandpa's face gets angry, his granddaughter is concerned that he doesn't love her anymore. But grandpa lets her know that even though his face changes, he still loves her very much.

Hall, Donald. *Ox-Cart Man.* New York: The Viking Press, 1979.

A wonderfully written Caldecott Medal book with illustrations by Barbara Cooney. Into the ox-cart go all the delicious foods that the family has grown, as well as the things they have made to sell at market.

Hazen, Barbara Shook. *Tight Times.* New York: Puffin Books, 1983.

Tight economic times mean a little boy can't have a dog. When dad loses his job, the family faces an even tougher battle. Thanks to a little orphan kitten and a human sandwich hug, the family pulls together through tight times to better times. Featured on PBS "Reading Rainbow."

Hazen, Barbara Shook. *Why Can't You Stay Home with Me?* New York: Golden Books, 1986.

Because Melissa's mother works, life is better in lots of ways, but it's tougher in some ways too. This story can help daycare teachers explain to preschoolers the advantages of having mom work outside the home.

Hazen, Barbara Shook. *Why Couldn't I Be an Only Kid Like You, Wigger.* New York: Atheneum, 1975.

Wigger has it made because he's an only child, says his friend. Trouble is, says Wigger, it gets lonely being an only child.

Hedderwick, Mairi. *Katie Morag and the Two Grandmothers.* Boston: Little, Brown, 1987.

Granma Mainland and Grannie Island are as different as different can be, but both are loved by Katie Morag, their granddaughter.

Hest, Amy. *The Mommy Exchange.* New York: Macmillan, 1991.

Jason wants noise and messy, and his friend Jessica wants quiet and neat. Together they hatch a plan to switch mommies—at least for a weekend.

Hines, Anna Grossnickle. *Daddy Makes the Best Spaghetti.* New York: Clarion Books, 1986.

Special moments between a dad and his son come at dinner time, bath time, and bedtime in this touching story.

Hurd, Thacher. *Mama Don't Allow.* New York: Harper & Row, 1984.

Mom can't stand Miles practicing his saxophone in the house. He decides to form a swamp band so that he and his friends can play to their hearts' content. Featured on PBS "Reading Rainbow."

Johnston, Tony. *Grandpa's Song.* New York: Dial, 1991.

Grandpa's voice is loud as a lion when he bellows out the old favorite songs. But the best song is the one no one has heard yet—the one he has made up himself.

Keats, Ezra Jack. *Apt. 3.* London: Hamish Hamilton, 1971.

The haunting sound of a harmonica on a rainy day leads Sam on a chase through his apartment building to see who's playing it. When Sam finds the person, he's surprised how much the blind man knows.

Keats, Ezra Jack. *Peter's Chair.* New York: Harper & Row, 1967.

While mother fusses with the new baby, Peter watches his crib, high chair, and cradle being painted pink for his baby sister. He doesn't like it one bit!

Mayer, Mercer. *Just Shopping with Mom.* New York: Golden Books, 1989.

Shopping at a supermarket is one of the first adventures a child experiences. The events in this picture book will be familiar to preschoolers, and they'll discover it's a great way to share a weekly family tradition.

Meyers, Odette. *The Enchanted Umbrella.* San Diego: Harcourt Brace Jovanovich, 1988.

The old man and his assistant Patou make wonderful umbrellas. When the old man dies, his lazy and selfish nephew gives Patou an umbrella and tells him to leave. But the umbrella is magical!

Moore, Elaine. *Grandma's House.* New York: Lothrop, Lee and Shepard, 1985.

A three-day visit to Grandma's big, old house in the country is a special time for a little girl. There's time enough to plant trees, pick plums, and even eat ice cream in the mall.

Munsch, Robert. *Love You Forever.* Ontario: Firefly Books, 1986.

A mother's love is evident in this charming picture book. The adult reader can expect to shed a few tears in remembering his or her own childhood experiences.

Schwartz, Amy. *Bea and Mr. Jones.* New York: Puffin Books, 1982.

Bea's had it with kindergarten and Mr. Jones isn't crazy about his job, either. So they switch and love their new work assignments!

Scott, Ann Herbert. *Grandmother's Chair.* New York: Clarion Books, 1990.

The little black and gold chair that grandmother had as a young girl makes its way through three generations of the family album pictures and will mostly likely be around for at least three more. This picture book points out the importance of family heirlooms.

Sendak, Maurice. *Where the Wild Things Are.* New York: Scholastic, 1963.

Mother calls Max "wild thing" and sends him to bed. In his room he takes a fantasy journey to where the real wild things are.

Spinelli, Eileen. *Thanksgiving at the Tappletons'.* New York: J.B. Lippincott, 1982.

A big turkey dinner is really not what Thanksgiving's all about, as the Tappletons find out.

Sharmat, Marjorie Weinman. *Gila Monsters Meet You at the Airport.* New York: Macmillan, 1980.

Back East, people don't know what it's really like to live out West. They think a Gila monster might meet them at the airport! This book describes the fears a young boy faces as he gets ready to move across country. Featured on PBS "Reading Rainbow."

Yolen, Jane. *Owl Moon.* New York: Philomel Books, 1987.

It's the simple rituals that most often bond parents with their children. In this family, owling is one such ritual, and dad turns it into a very important lesson in hope. A Caldecott Medal winner, featured on PBS "Reading Rainbow."

Zolotow, Charlotte. *Big Sister and Little Sister.* New York: Harper & Row, 1966.

Big sisters are nice because they take care of their little sisters. Sometimes, however, little sisters get tired of being told what to do. Big sister's tears convince little sister that caring for each other is what it's all about.

Zolotow, Charlotte. *My Grandson Lew.* New York: Harper & Row, 1974.

Lewis remembers his grandpa, even though the man died four years ago when Lewis was small. Among the things he misses are "eye hugs" and being carried.

Families Snacktime

Little Trees

Here's an idea that expands the "family tree" theme and also will encourage children to try a new food. Typically children don't like the taste of cooked broccoli because of its strong flavor. However, uncooked broccoli has a different taste and texture. It is good dipped in a variety of sauces, including soft cream cheese. Serve with crackers for a complete snack.

Families Game

Family Guessing Game

Children take turns describing a member of their family while the others guess who is being described. Movement clues as well as verbal clues can be used. For example: One child might give clues to his father's occupation as a firefighter, as well as verbal clues such as, "He lives in my house and he is not my mom."

Teacher note: Encourage every child to participate.

Shield for Coat of Arms

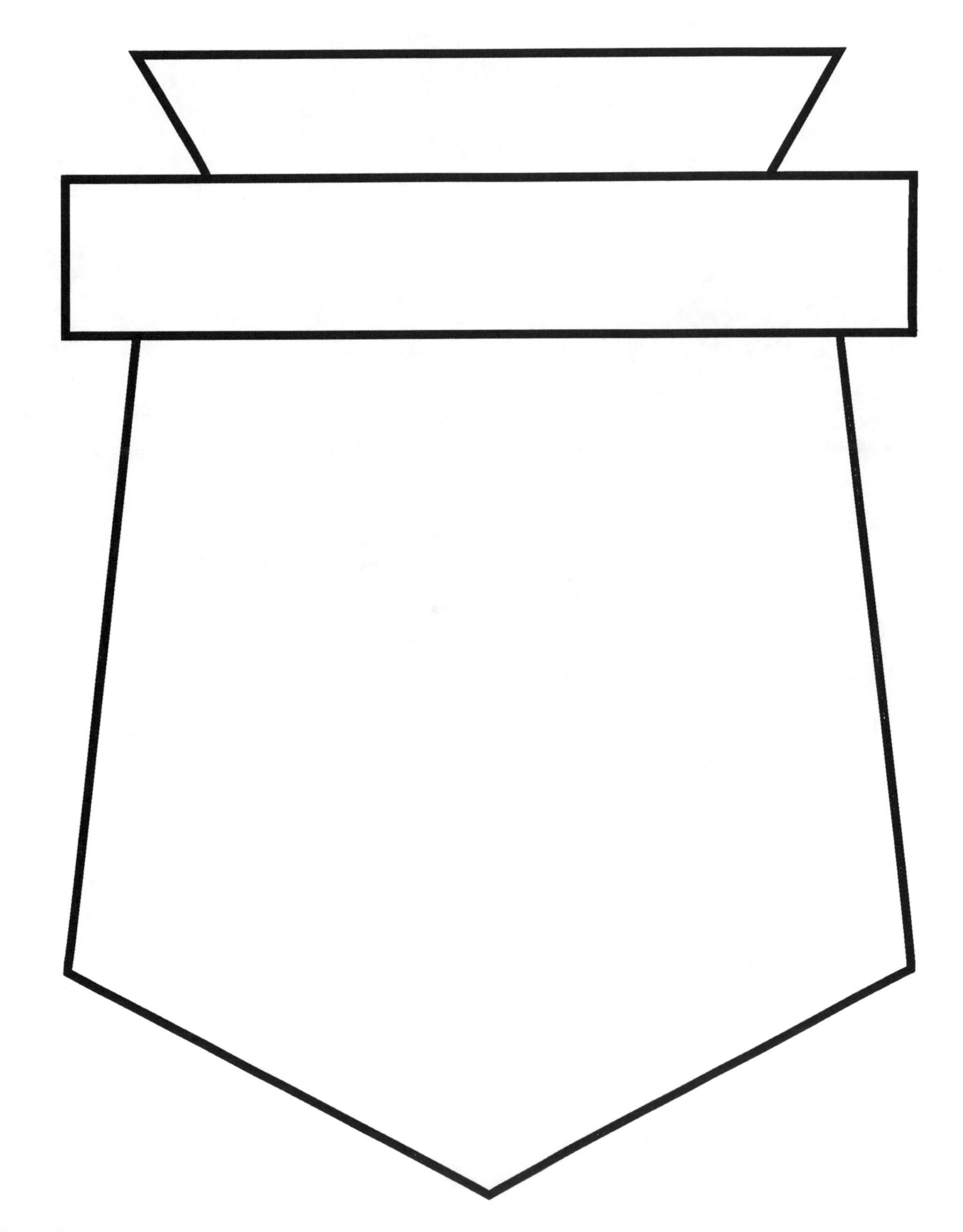

Cheerful Chums

Friendships are important to children, but they evolve in stages. This development can be seen while observing children play. Initially, a child's play is called "onlooking" as the infant watches other children playing. Next, the child progresses to "solitary," then "parallel," and "associative" play stages. In these three stages, the child still does not fully interact with other children. Finally, in the "cooperative" stage of play, the child is a participant in a structured activity with rules and a part for each child to play. From this stage, friendships are born—many of which last a lifetime.

Cheerful Chums BodyArt recognizes that the children need to progress sequentially through each stage of play. The projects enable the child to develop positive self-esteem and facilitate a smooth transition from one stage to the next.

"Stepping Out With My Friends" Bulletin Board

There's nothing better when you're little than to walk arm-in-arm with a friend. This BodyArt project enables your children to step out with all their friends.

Use bulletin board paper for the background. In the upper left-hand corner, attach a school picture, and in the lower right-hand corner a park picture (see the reproducibles at the end of this chapter). Then trace each child's shoe onto construction paper and cut out.

If desired, have the children color or personalize their shoes with nontoxic markers or crayons. Glue the paper shoes to the bulletin board in a zigzag pattern to represent feet walking from school to the park.

Hand Shaker

Materials: 9-inch paper plates, popcorn (unpopped), hole puncher, ribbons, stapler, scissors, construction paper, nontoxic glue, nontoxic washable markers.

Make music with friends and give new meaning to the term "handshake" with this BodyArt hand shaker. Each shaker is made of two 9-inch paper plates stapled together around the edges. Leave a small opening to add popcorn, then finish stapling shut.

Trace both child's hands (fingers open) on construction paper and cut out. Then glue onto paper plate, placing the left hand on one side of the shaker and the right hand on the other side.

Have the children personalize their hand shakers by decorating with markers. Punch holes around the edges and tie ribbons through holes to add interest when moving hand shakers to music.

Friendship Bracelet

Materials: elastic string, paper grocery bags, dry macaroni (short and large-holed), rubbing alcohol, food coloring, plastic stirrers, plastic bowls.

Children love friendship bracelets. They are easy to make, and the process helps develop small motor skills. First, put a cup of macaroni into a plastic bowl (one bowl for each color used). Add about one to two teaspoons of rubbing alcohol to noodles and stir. Mixture should be slightly moist but not wet. Add one to two drops of food coloring and stir again. Pour the macaroni of each color into a separate brown bag and fold to close at top. Shake until macaroni is dry.

Then distribute one 12-inch piece of elastic string to each child and demonstrate how to thread the macaroni. Allow the children to choose their own colors and create their own patterns to personalize each friendship bracelet. When the desired length has been obtained, tie securely and cut off excess string.

Teacher note: Wrap tape around one end of the string to allow for easier threading of macaroni. To prevent macaroni from "slipping through," thread and tie one piece at the bottom of each string.

The rubbing alcohol is used to help set the colors. It quickly evaporates and will be completely gone when the children are working with the dry macaroni.

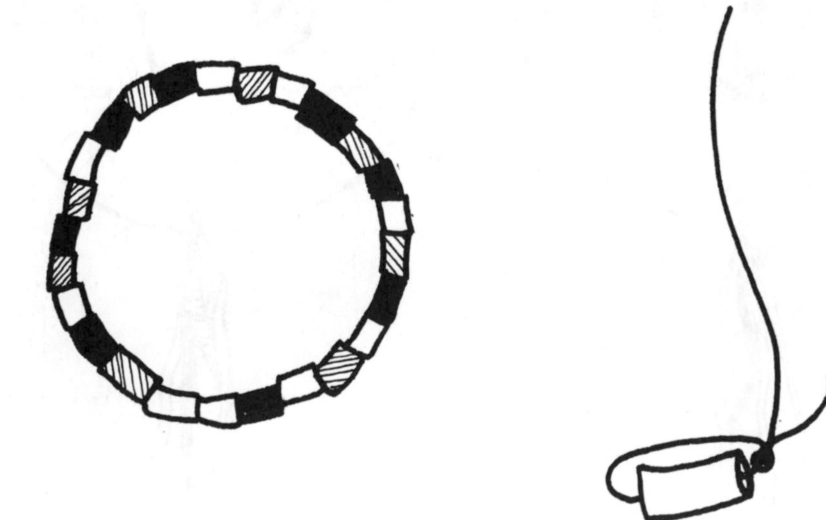

Friendly Handprint Wrapping Paper

Materials: large roll of white butcher paper or newsprint, scissors, nontoxic tempera paint. Optional: boxes.

Handprint wrapping paper can be used to wrap a gift—maybe a friendship bracelet you have made—to give to a special friend.

Spread a large sheet of white paper out on a table. Have children take turns dipping their hands into tempera paint in a variety of colors and making prints on the paper. When all the prints are dry, cut the paper into pieces, giving each child enough to wrap a present for a friend.

Friendship Bouquet

Materials: construction paper in a variety of colors, nontoxic washable markers, 12-inch pipe cleaners, scissors, stapler, Styrofoam ball or square (found in craft stores) to fit bottom of flower vase, vase (large, shallow vase works best). Optional: feathers.

Here the children make a flower arrangement with their friends as a symbol of the beauty they can create by working together.

To make a group friendship bouquet, trace each child's hand (fingers open) on construction paper and cut out. Fold over so that paper thumb and pinky finger meet. Stick a pipe cleaner through the base of the paper hand and staple to attach. Then place the Styrofoam into the bottom of the vase. Stick each hand flower into the Styrofoam and arrange into a bouquet. If desired, feathers can be added to represent foliage.

This project can be used as a centerpiece to highlight your Cheerful Chums unit. When the unit is complete, allow the children to claim their individual flowers and take them home.

Teacher note: Any container can be substituted for a vase. Round metal tins work especially well and are unbreakable.

Cheerful Chums Finger Play and Movement Song

Finger Friends

Finger friends wiggle,
and finger friends drum.
Finger friends play the flute,
and sometimes strum!

Finger friends help me eat
and brush my teeth at night.
Finger friends brush my hair
and shade my eyes from light.

Finger friends help me catch
a ball that's far away.
Finger friends help me hug
on any lonely day.

Teacher note: Hands keep busy in this finger play that has children "making music" and doing other more familiar activities.

The Handshake Song

(Sung to "Baa, Baa, Black Sheep")

Shake, shake, handshake,
Have you any friends?
Yes sir, yes ma'am,
Shake my hand.

Teacher note: Children stand in a circle. Designate a starter. Each child in turn shakes hands with the neighboring child while everyone sings or chants the verse. Continue all the way around the circle.

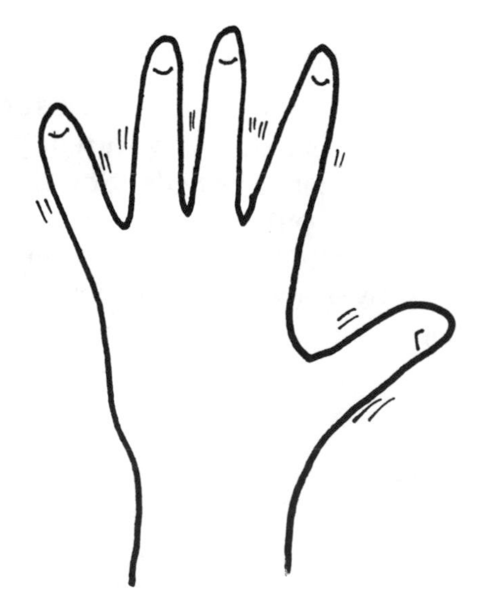

Cheerful Chums Read-Alouds

Fiction Picture Books

Aliki. *We Are Best Friends.* New York: Trumpet Club, 1982.

Spyro and Stelio are best friends who have to face a crisis when one of them moves away.

Bayer, Jane. *A My Name Is Alice.* New York: Dial Books for Young Readers, 1984.

Alice is just one of the friends children will meet in this wonderful alphabet book. Long ago children made up their own A for Alice song. Children today can enjoy making their own alphabet books, even though they can't spell. Have them dictate their books into a tape recorder.

Bornstein, Ruth Lercher. *The Seedling Child.* San Diego, CA: Harcourt Brace Jovanovich, 1987.

A girl picks up a tiny seed on the ground and finds a child inside. Beautifully illustrated, poetic picture book that tells the story of a special "feel good" friend.

Cooney, Nancy Evans. *The Blanket That Had to Go.* New York: G.P. Putnam's Sons, 1981.

Susi's blanket is her special friend. When she finds out she can't bring it to kindergarten, she thinks of all sorts of ways to disguise it. Finally a solution is found.

Delton, Judy. *Two Good Friends.* New York: Crown, 1974.

Duck and bear are an odd pair of friends. Duck has a need to clean; bear's sloppy kitchen has the warm, good smell of nut pies cooking. Both find the friendship worthwhile and genuine.

Ets, Marie Hall. *Play With Me.* New York: Puffin Books, 1976.

A little girl goes out to the meadow to find a friend to play with in this Caldecott Honor book. At first it doesn't look as if she'll find anyone. Then suddenly they all come back—frog, rabbit, fawn, chipmunk, snake, and blue jay—and the little girl has loads of new friends!

Fitzhugh, Louise. *Bang, Bang, You're Dead.* New York: Harper Collins, 1969.

Conflict between friends is tough on children. In this story, two boys learn the value of friendship when they decide to share a hill rather than fight over it.

Fox, Memo. *Wilfrid Gordon McDonald Partridge.* New York: Kane/Miller, 1985.

This story explores the special friendship between a little boy and an older woman in the nursing home next door. The only thing they have in common is that they both have four names—but this one bond is enough to help Miss Nancy find her memory again.

Glen, Maggie. *Ruby.* New York: G.P. Putnam's Sons, 1990.

Ruby is on the toy store's back shelf because she's a mistake—a teddy bear with a toy leopard's body. She thinks the S on her paw means special, not second, and to the little girl who buys her, Ruby is a very special friend indeed.

Mahy, Margaret. *The Boy Who Was Followed Home.* New York: Dial Books for Young Readers, 1975.

Robert is an ordinary boy with an extraordinary friend—the hippopotamus who follows him home. His parents are not so delighted, especially when the hippo brings more hippo friends home to visit.

Mayer, Mercer. *Little Critter's This Is My Friend.* New York: Golden Books, 1989.

Friends are there through thick and thin, in spite of tricks and mad days.

Viorst, Judith. *The Tenth Good Thing About Barney.* New York: Macmillan, 1971.

When Barney the cat dies, it is a sad day for the little boy who cared for him—but the child's parents help him remember all of the good times he shared with Barney. This book can help youngsters cope with (and better understand) the death of a pet.

Walter, Mildred Pitts. *Ty's One-Man Band.* New York: Scholastic, 1980.

Everyone's too busy to play with Ty except for Andro, the one-man band who comes to town at night to play music for the entire community.

Williams, Margery. *The Velveteen Rabbit.* New York: Avon Books, 1975.

Friendship between a boy and his velveteen rabbit is so full of love that the bunny is granted its dearest wish—to become real.

Zolotow, Charlotte. *The New Friend.* New York: Thomas Y. Crowell, 1968.

It's tough for a child to see a special friend playing with someone else. This book can help your preschoolers who have felt sad when this happens to them.

Cheerful Chums Snacktime

Friendship Salad

Remember the story of "Stone Soup"? Starting with only a stone, everyone contributes something to make a tasty soup. Friendship salad produces the same kind of results without cooking. Encourage each child to bring one unpeeled, uncut piece of fruit. As a group, children can peel and cut the fruit with supervision. Mix and serve to each child.

Teacher note: As with any cooking project, be sure children's hands are clean. To ensure that a variety of fruit will be brought in, you might assign each child a favorite fruit. Encourage a variety, including kiwi, honeydew, and cantaloupe, and use these to extend your children's vocabulary skills.

Cheerful Chums Game

Sharing with My Friends

To encourage social skill development, have the children bring in a favorite stuffed animal or toy. Each child then trades toys with a friend. Set timer for a short amount of time (two minutes to begin with). When the timer rings, each child returns the toy to its owner. As children grow more comfortable with the concept of sharing, repeat the game and extend the time.

School Picture

Park Picture

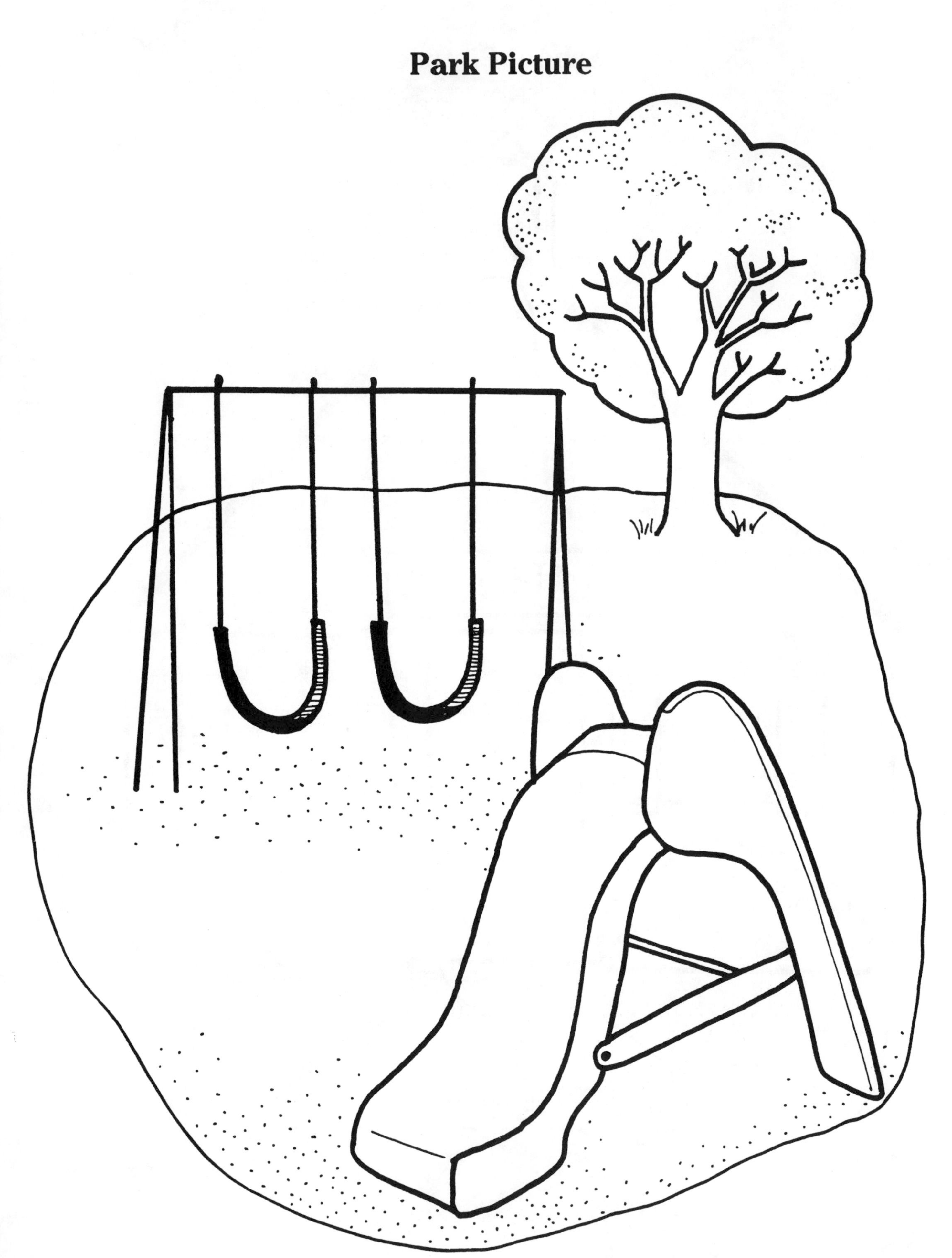

Crackerjack Communities

Children's sense of community begins to grow as soon as they become aware that their family's physical survival is dependent upon the outside world. Through symbols, the child learns to associate what help is available—from the sign at the corner bus stop to the familiar trademarks of grocery stores and fast-food chains. These first symbol associations are actually reading readiness skills and should be encouraged by parents and teachers alike.

The sirens of fire trucks, ambulances, and police cars going by are reminders of the need for community helpers to ensure the children's safety. A child's dramatic play often reflects an interest in and appreciation for such helpers that may turn into a commitment for a lifetime career.

Crackerjack Communities BodyArt projects acknowledge this awareness and interest, enriching the children's lives by helping them appreciate the world around them.

"When I Grow Up" Bulletin Board

Children often set lifetime goals at a very early age. This is reinforced by adults who, after asking a child how old she is, will then ask, "What do you want to be when you grow up?" This bulletin board will help children explore possible goals as they identify with community helpers and workers.

This display works in tandem with the Career Feet BodyArt project, which you will need to do first. To set up the display, attach several strips of Velcro (soft side) horizontally across the board. Next attach a spot of Velcro (loop side) to the top back of the BodyArt Career Feet the children have made. Place the paper feet on the Velcro strips, grouping those with similar career choices. Allow children to make career changes whenever they wish.

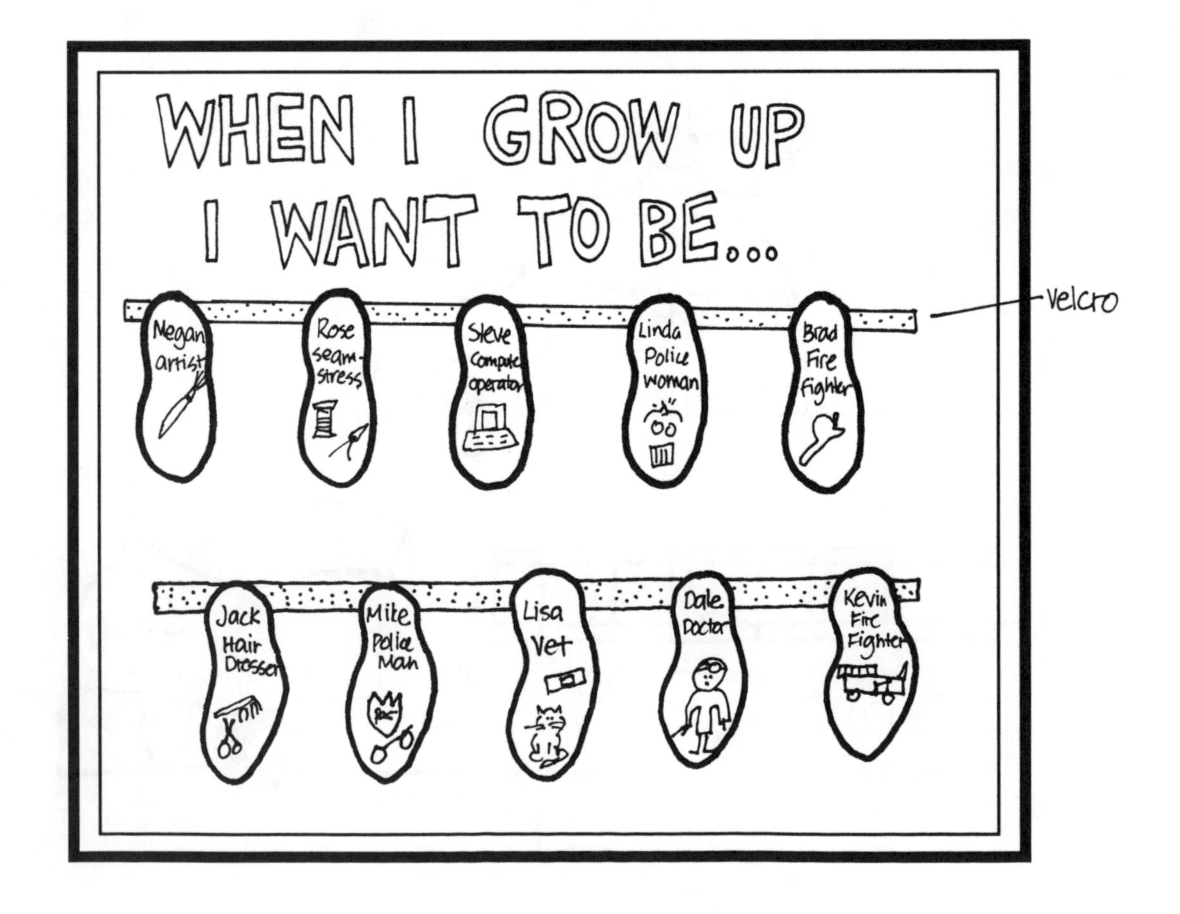

Handy Shield

Materials: tagboard, crayons, scissors, safety pin or nontoxic glue, construction paper for wallet.

Community workers often display a badge to proudly identify their chosen occupation. This BodyArt project gives each child a badge that can be displayed on a hat or on clothing, or one that can be carried in a folded piece of paper that represents a wallet.

To make each handy shield, trace the child's hand on a piece of tagboard (fingers and thumb closed) and cut out. Color with crayons and label as desired (fingers pointing downward are the bottom of the badge). Add a safety pin or glue into folded paper wallets.

Career Feet

Materials: white tagboard, nontoxic washable markers, crayons, scissors, Velcro.

This project is to be used in conjunction with the "When I Grow Up" bulletin board. It allows children to role-play career choices. Start by discussing with the children various roles that community workers and helpers play. Then trace each child's shoe on tagboard and cut out.

Draw in facial features and color or decorate appropriately depending on the child's career choice. Attach a piece of Velcro (loop side) to the top back of each foot.

Teacher note: Encourage children to participate in dramatic play with their career feet. The bulletin board can serve as a "stage" on which children play out their fantasies.

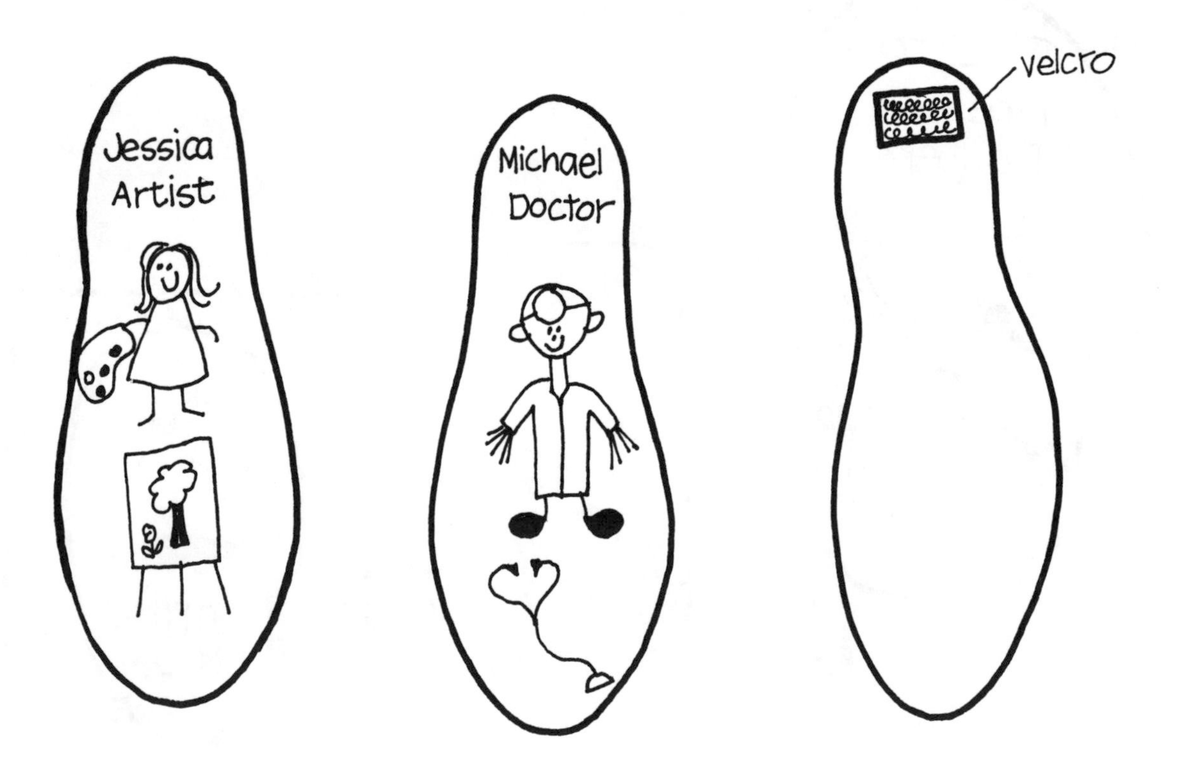

Stop and Go Sign

Materials: white tagboard, green and red nontoxic tempera paint, scissors, tongue depressors, nontoxic glue. Optional: glue gun.

For safety reasons, parents like their children to recognize at an early age the colors associated with stop and go. This red-for-stop, green-for-go project can be used with the "Stop and Go Game" in this chapter to reinforce the safety concept.

Use the reproducible Sign Pattern (see the end of this chapter) to create a template and prepare an octagon-shaped tagboard sign for each child.

Glue a tongue depressor to each tagboard sign. Then have children dip one hand into red tempera paint and make a handprint (fingers open) on one side of the sign. When paint is dry, repeat on the reverse side using green paint.

Teacher note: A glue gun works especially well for affixing the handle. However, be careful when using around young children.

Communities Movement Songs

Sounds of the Town

(Sung to "Here We Go Round the Mulberry Bush")

This is the sound the fire trucks make,
fire trucks make, fire trucks make,
This is the sound the fire trucks make:
(Children make siren noise.)

This is the sound the librarian makes,
librarian makes, librarian makes,
This is the sound the librarian makes:
(Children make shushing noise.)

Additional verses:

This is the sound the garbage truck makes: (Clink, clank, clunk.)

This is the sound the school bell makes: (Ringggggggg.)

This is the sound the police car makes: (Rrrh, rrrh, rrrh.)

This is the sound of the ice cream truck: (Ding a ling, ding a ling.)

This is the sound the street sweeper makes: (Swish, swish, swish.)

This is the sound a delivery truck makes: (Beep, beep, beep.)

This is the sound the carpenter makes: (Bam, bam, bam.)

This is the sound the barber makes: (Snip, snip, buzzzzzz.)

Teacher note: This song can be used with the read-aloud *City Sounds* by Rebecca Emberley.

Clean-Up Song

(Sung to "Twinkle, Twinkle, Little Star")

Now it's time to pick up toys,
Girls can do it, so can boys.
Into baskets, onto shelves,
We can clean up by ourselves.
Now it's time to pick up toys,
Girls can do it, so can boys.

Now it's time to pick up toys,
Girls can do it, so can boys.
Paints and crayons, balls and games,
Jig-saw puzzles in their frames.
Now it's time to pick up toys,
Girls can do it, so can boys.

Now it's time to pick up toys.
Girls can do it, so can boys.
Cars and dolls and blocks and books,
See how tidy our room looks.
Now it's time to pick up toys,
Girls can do it, so can boys.

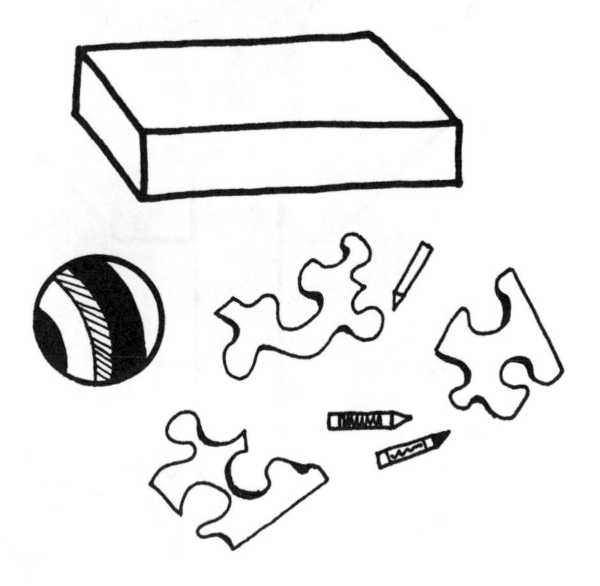

Communities Read-Alouds

Fiction Picture Books

Barbour, Karen. *Little Nino's Pizzeria.* San Diego, CA: Harcourt Brace Jovanovich, 1987.

Sometimes bigger isn't necessarily better as Nino finds out when he turns his popular pizzeria into a fancy restaurant. Wonderfully illustrated. A Parents' Choice Honors book featured on PBS "Reading Rainbow."

Bax, Martin. *Edmond Went Far Away.* San Diego, CA: Harcourt Brace Jovanovich, 1988.

Farmyard friends and community are detailed in this picture book with Edmond as the young hero who, like many children, loves to explore and discover.

Burton, Virginia Lee. *Mike Mulligan and His Steam Shovel.* Boston: Houghton Mifflin, 1967.

An oldy but goody, Mike Mulligan's steam shovel looks a lot like the construction equipment used today to build homes, skyscrapers, and roads in the community.

Carle, Eric. *Pancakes! Pancakes!* New York: Alfred A. Knopf, 1970.

Pancakes take a lot of work to make as you'll discover in this wonderfully illustrated book that teaches children as much about the community as about pancakes.

Carle, Eric. *Walter the Baker.* New York: Alfred A. Knopf, 1972.

This is an old story retold and illustrated with bold tissue-paper collages. Walter is the best baker in town until one day he runs out of milk and bakes the worst rolls ever! To redeem himself, he has to make a new creation. The result is delicious!

Cooney, Barbara. *Island Boy.* New York: Trumpet Club Special Edition, 1988.

A young boy's childhood memories are full of endearing family traditions,

Hest, Amy. *The Purple Coat.* New York: Four Winds Press, 1986.

This year Gabby wants a purple coat from her Grampa's tailor shop instead of her usual navy blue coat. When Gabby's mother protests, Grampa reminds her that she once wanted a tangerine dress. They finally settle on a coat that pleases everyone!

Howe, James. *The Day the Teacher Went Bananas.* New York: E.P. Dutton, 1984.

All the children want to be like the new teacher. The only trouble is, the new teacher is a monkey.

Jonas, Ann. *Round Trip.* New York: Greenwillow Books, 1983.

Stunning black-and-white silhouettes portray the different environments to be seen on a day trip from the country to the city. For the return trip, you look at the same magical pictures upside down and backward.

Maiorano, Robert and Rachel Isadora. *Backstage.* New York: Greenwillow Books, 1978.

This informative book follows Olivia as she takes readers behind the scenes of a stage performance until she finally finds the costume department where her mother works.

Noble, Trinka Hakes. *Meanwhile Back at the Ranch.* New York: Dial Books for Young Readers, 1987.

This timeless tale of rancher Hicks will delight country and city readers alike. Featured on PBS "Reading Rainbow."

Pinkwater, Daniel. *Tooth-Gnasher Superflash.* New York: Four Winds Press, 1981.

The Popsnorkles new car does so many neat things that it's no wonder the family falls in love with this Detroit dandy. Featured on PBS "Reading Rainbow."

Provensen, Alice and Martin. *Shaker Lane.* New York: The Trumpet Club, 1987.

Wonderfully illustrated, the story of Shaker Lane reaffirms the values of family heritage and community involvement.

Slobodkina, Esphyr. *Caps For Sale.* New York: Harper & Row, 1968.

Children especially like this old favorite because it includes lots of monkey business. It's a good book for children to act out, wearing actual caps.

Zemach, Harve. *The Judge.* Toronto: Collins, 1969.

This Caldecott Honor book weaves the tale of prisoners who try to tell the judge about a horrible thing coming this way. The judge won't believe the prisoners until it's too late!

Nonfiction

Brown, David. *Someone Always Needs a Policeman.* New York: Simon & Schuster, 1972.

Police officers are nice to have around in the community as preschoolers will discover in this picture book.

Emberley, Rebecca. *City Sounds.* Boston: Little, Brown, 1989.

Children learn all about the different sounds you can hear in the city—sounds made by wheels, radios, and those who make their living there.

Faulkner, Keith. *First Questions About Transport.* Kent, England: Hodder and Stoughton, 1983.

Trains of the future, flying machines without power, vehicles that save lives—it's all here for older preschoolers to learn about.

Rice, Eve. *City Night.* New York: Greenwillow Books, 1987.

The community comes alive during this special city night.

Scarry, Richard. *Cars and Trucks and Things That Go.* Racine, WI: Western Publishing, 1974.

Here's an imaginative blend of fact and fantasy that'll tickle little funnybones. All sorts of cars and trucks are described, with a focus on the traditional varieties—garbage trucks, excavators, and ditchdiggers—but with the occasional bananamobile or goldbug dump truck thrown in just for fun.

Communities Snacktime

Neighborhood Pizzerias

The pizzeria is a delicious addition to most communities. The read-aloud *Little Nino's Pizzeria* by Karen Barbour is a wonderful introduction to preparing and enjoying this snack.

Use refrigerated biscuit dough found in your neighborhood food store. Flatten the dough and spread with pizza sauce. Add toppings of your choice and cheese. Bake according to package directions and enjoy personal pizzas.

Communities Game

Stop and Go Game

Use your BodyArt stop-and-go sign in this version of a traditional game.

The children take turns being the safety patrol and holding their stop and go signs while the other children follow their directions. When the green side is shown, children can move forward. When the red side is shown, they stop.

This game reinforces street safety skills.

Sign Pattern

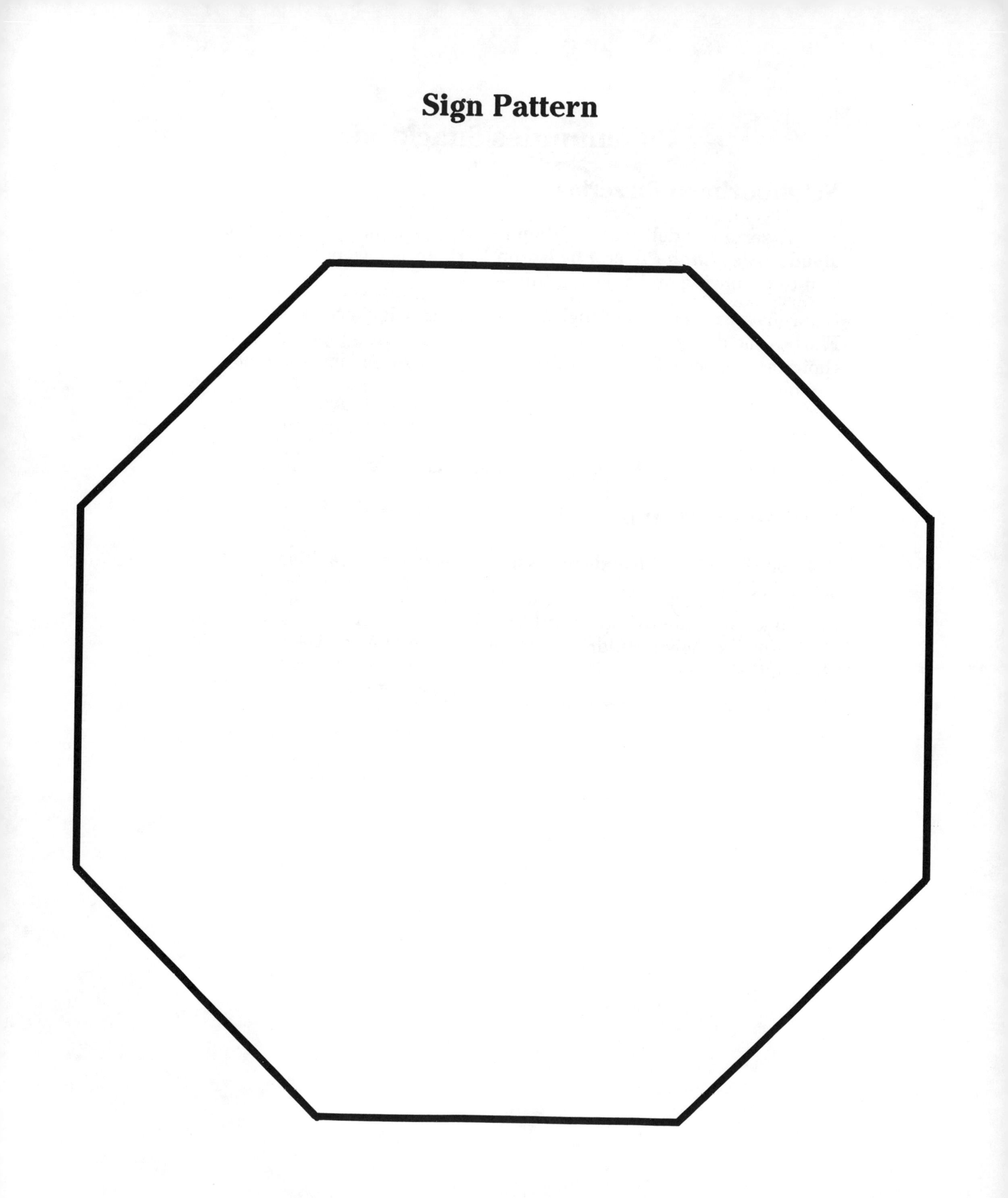

Going Global

Smiles, tears, and laughter are common to all children no matter where they live. The BodyArt projects in this global unit give children a taste of other cultures around the world.

The large continent of Africa contains many countries and a rich and diverse climate—from the Sahara desert in the northernmost part, to the equatorial tropical rain forests. Africa's people, too, represent a wide variety of different cultures that stem back thousands of years.

In Asia, there's mysterious China, which was for so long isolated and protected from Western influence. Now that the "gates are open" for international learning, we are exposed to exotic traditions and customs that are full of wonderful surprises.

Finally, in the many Spanish-speaking countries of the Western Hemisphere we get a glimpse of all the power and majesty of the Hispanic culture. The geography, music, artwork, and festivals of these countries open up a variety of new experiences—from overflowing volcanoes to joyous piñata celebrations.

For all the differences among the various nationalities, we need to remember that people the world around are much like ourselves. An appropriate theme song for this unit would be "It's a Small World" by Richard M. Sherman and Robert B. Sherman, familiar to many people from its use in the Disneyland attraction featuring dolls in the dress of different nations.

"Hands From Other Lands" Bulletin Board

The world is an enormous place, with more than 5 billion people. Celebrate the people of this planet with a bulletin board that combines the familiar (children's hands) with the exotic (pictures of other lands).

You'll need magazine pictures or travel agency brochures to make a collage border representing different countries of the world. Cut out a large blue circle to represent the earth and hang in the center of your bulletin board.

Trace the children's hands on construction paper in a wide range of skin tones—pinks, tans, yellow, browns, black—to depict physical differences in coloring. Cut out and position each hand within the blue globe.

"The Planet Song" in this chapter ties in nicely with this bulletin board.

Overflowing Volcano

Materials: brown lunch-sized paper bag, scissors, newspaper for stuffing, red construction paper, stapler, nontoxic washable markers.

In many Spanish-speaking countries in Central and South America, active volcanoes are very much a part of daily life. You might introduce this project with the read-aloud *Hill of Fire* by Thomas Lewis.

To make each volcano, trace the child's hand on red construction paper and cut out. This will represent lava erupting from the top of the volcano. Stuff a brown lunch-sized paper bag with wadded up newspaper. Position the lava hand at the top of the volcano (fingers pointing up) and staple closed.

Children can then add embellishments, such as red lava flows down the sides of the bag, with nontoxic washable markers.

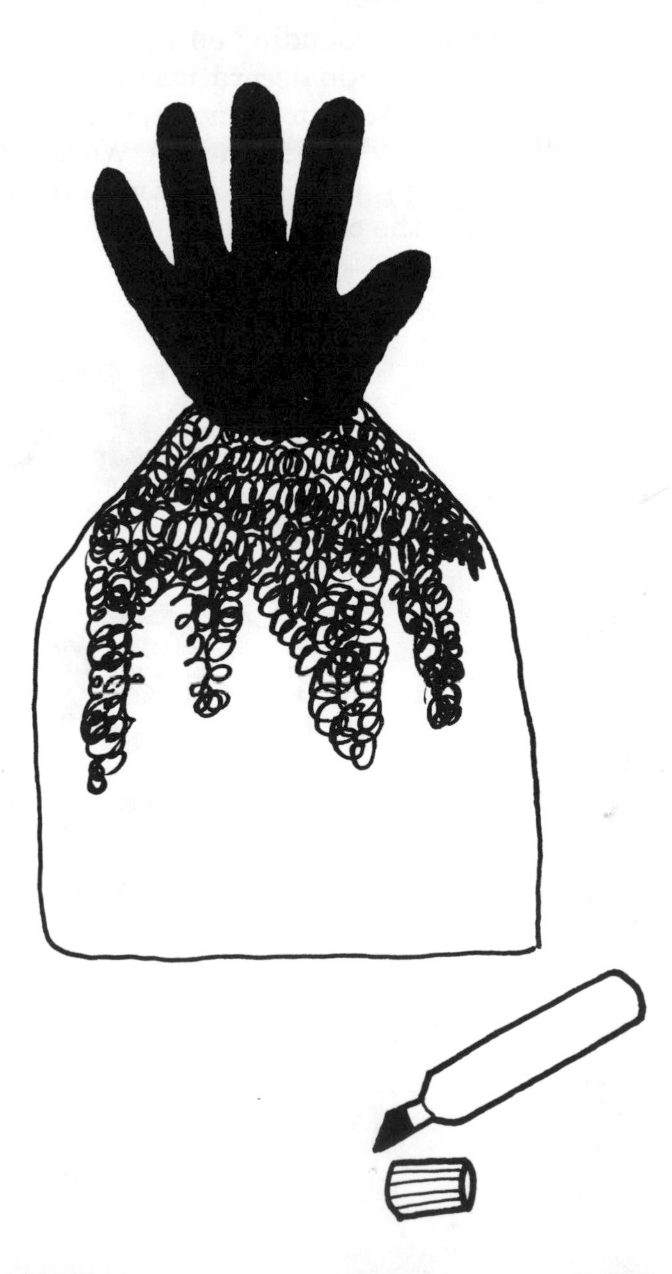

Ceremonial Face Masks

Materials: nontoxic washable markers, 9-inch paper plates, scissors, tongue depressors, nontoxic glue, decorative ribbon or yarn, construction paper.

In many cultures around the world, from Africa to the South Seas, masks are worn during ceremonies and rituals.

To make a simple face mask, cut eye holes in each paper plate to enable the child to see through the mask. Next, have the children draw in facial features. Trace children's hands on construction paper and cut out. Position paper hands around the edges of the paper plate to look like hair, beard, or ears, depending on position and whether paper fingers are pointing up, down, or sideways. Then glue in place. Attach tongue depressor to bottom back of the paper plate. Add decorative ribbon or yarn as desired.

Teacher note: Depending on your age group and the materials available, you might add decorative items such as beads and sequins. However, children need to be monitored carefully when they are handling small and "tasty" looking items. We do NOT recommend glitter with this BodyArt project since glitter on the paper mask might come in contact with the child's eyes.

United Nations Parade

Materials: tagboard in a variety of colors, scissors, nontoxic washable markers, fabric, trimmings, beads, yarn, hole puncher, nontoxic glue. Optional: glue gun.

Have a United Nations parade any time of the year and let your children's fingers do the walking for their people of different cultures.

To make the people for the parade, trace each child's foot (shoes on) on a piece of tagboard. Cut out. Add two holes near the bottom of the heel, starting with a hole puncher and then cutting big enough and positioned so that the child's index and middle finger can slip comfortably through the holes. The child's fingers will become the legs of someone in the parade.

Decorate each paper person, drawing in facial features and arms and hands, and gluing bits of fabric, yarn, and trimmings to represent colorful costumes of different world cultures. Ribbons and streamers will add a festive appearance.

Have the children march their parade people around, singing "The Children of the World" song provided in this chapter.

International Finger Fans

Materials: recyclable manila folders or any heavier weight paper, nontoxic washable markers or crayons, stapler, scissors, nontoxic glue, tongue depressors. Optional: glue gun.

Here's a BodyArt project that crosses international borders and can be used to celebrate a variety of cultures, although the decorative style and materials will differ. Give your children an opportunity to choose which culture they'd like to portray with their finger fans. Chinese fans will be decorated with birds and flowers. Spanish fans will have a black or white lacy style. African fans will be simpler in style, using natural colors to represent grass or straw.

To make each finger fan, trace each child's hand (fingers together) five or six times on a manila folder or heavier colored paper. Staple together to form an open fan. Attach tongue depressor with glue and decorate with markers or crayons.

Teacher note: A glue gun will help you finish the projects faster. Make sure the gun is kept out of children's reach.

Hand Flags

Materials: white tagboard, scissors, nontoxic washable markers or crayons, tongue depressors, glue, copies of Flags reproducibles for reference (see end of this chapter).

The bright colors and patterns of flags appeal even to young children and can spark an early interest in world geography.

Trace each child's hand (fingers and thumb together) on a piece of white tagboard. Cut out, then draw in lines and shapes to represent the flag design of their choice. Have the children color appropriately. Glue tongue depressor to side of hand to put each flag on a pole.

Teacher note: If you want to give the children a broader range of choices than is provided for the Flag Matching game, many almanacs, atlases, dictionaries, or encyclopedias have full pages picturing national flags from around the world.

Global Rhyme and Movement Song

Spinning World

Our world is spinning
round and round and never does
it stop.
It's spinning through the heavens
like a big, blue top.

Teacher note: With this rhyme, children spin their whole body, just like the world. They can spin while standing, while crouching and holding their knees, and while sitting on the floor.

The Planet Song

(sung to "Yellow Submarine")

We all live on a lovely, big planet
lovely, big planet,
lovely, big planet
We all live on a lovely, big planet
that's small enough for me.

The Children of the World

(Sung to "The Farmer in the Dell")

The children of the world,
The children of the world,
We want to celebrate
The children of the world.

Some come from Mexico
And Puerto Rico too,
Some come from sunny Spain,
From Chile, and Peru.

Some come from old Taiwan
And mountains in Tibet,
Some come from Singapore—
All friends we've never met.

Some come from Africa,
A great, enormous land,
Some from the Middle East
Come join our happy band.

No matter where they live,
No matter what they do,
We celebrate the children
In all we say and do.

Teacher note: This is a marching song for use with the BodyArt United Nations Parade.

Global Read-Alouds

Fiction Picture Books

Aardema, Verna. *Bringing the Rain to Kapiti Plain.* New York: Dial Books for Young Readers, 1981.

A Nandi tale that tells how Ki-pat brings the much-needed rain with his bow and arrow. Featured on PBS "Reading Rainbow."

Aardema, Verna. *Why Mosquitoes Buzz in People's Ears.* New York: Dial Press, 1975.

This West African tale includes exotic creatures your preschoolers may not have heard of, including an iguana, crow, and python.

Ada, Alma Flor. *The Gold Coin.* New York: Atheneum, 1991.

An old woman's kindness helps Juan the thief change his ways in this beautifully illustrated read-aloud.

Baker, Keith. *The Magic Fan.* San Diego, CA: Harcourt Brace Jovanovich, 1989.

Yoshi is a builder who wants to build something that goes beyond his small village. When he finds a magic fan he starts building again—just in time to save the village from the dreaded tsunami.

Bang, Molly. *The Paper Crane.* New York: Trumpet Club, 1985.

A restaurant owner's kindness to a penniless old man is repaid in a very special and magical way.

Bishop. Claire Hutchet. *The Five Chinese Brothers.* New York: Coward-McCann, 1938.

Five Chinese brothers all look alike but they each have special talents that help save one brother's life.

Brown, Marcia. *Shadow.* New York: Macmillan, 1982.

The dancing image of Shadow is brought to life by storytellers sitting around the fire in African villages. In connection with this Caldecott Medal offering, let children create their own shadows on the walls indoors or outside in the sun.

Demi. *The Empty Pot.* New York: Henry Holt, 1990.

Ping's honesty is rewarded even though he offers the emperor an empty pot instead of a beautiful bouquet.

Demi. *Liang and The Magic Paintbrush.* New York: Henry Holt, 1980.

No one will teach Liang to paint because he is poor. One night, though, Liang is given a magic paintbrush, and he creates so many wonderful things that even the emperor is envious.

Graham, Lorenz. *Hongry Catch the Foolish Boy.* New York: Thomas Y. Crowell, 1946.

Written in the idiom of people newly come to English speech, this Liberian tale catches the rhythm of an African storyteller and the beat of drums.

Haley, Gail E. *A Story A Story.* New York, 1970.

This Caldecott Medal winner retells an African tale of how, long ago, there were no stories on earth—until old Ananse, the Spider man, cleverly captured a leopard, a hornet, and a fairy to trade to Nyame, the Sky God, for his golden box full of stories.

Lewis, Thomas P. *Hill of Fire.* New York: Harper & Row, 1971.

Everyone else thinks their Mexican village has everything it needs, but the farmer isn't happy with his sleepy town where nothing ever happens. Then something happens that changes everything—El Monstruo! Featured on PBS "Reading Rainbow."

Louie, Ai-Ling. *Yeh-Shen.* New York: Philomel Books, 1982.

Ed Young's beautiful illustrations make this "Cinderella" story that dates back to the T'ang dynasty particularly vivid and memorable.

Martel, Cruz. *Yagua Days.* New York: Dial Press, 1976.

Adan lives in a Hispanic neighborhood in New York. On his first visit to relatives in Puerto Rico, he learns at last why his family calls rainy days "yagua days." Spanish word list is provided for enrichment learning.

Mosel, Arlene. *Tikki Tikki Tembo.* New York: Scholastic, 1968.

Once it was an honor to be the first-born son in a Chinese family, and he was given the longest name. This story tells why the Chinese changed this tradition and decided to give all their children short names instead of long ones.

Seeger, Pete. *Abiyoyo.* New York: Macmillan, 1986.

Adapted from an old South African lullaby and folk song, this story is about a little ukulele-playing boy and his magician father, both of whom are cast out of town for being so annoying. Then one day Abiyoyo—a giant who could eat people—frightens the town, and only the boy and his father know how to make the giant disappear.

Steptoe, John. *Mufaro's Beautiful Daughters.* New York: Lothrop, Lee and Shepard, 1987.

This African tale about Manyara and Nyasha is a triumph of kindness over greed, with beautiful illustrations.

Surat, Michele Maria. *Angel Child, Dragon Child.* New York: Scholastic, 1983.

Nguyen Hoa is affectionately called Ut by her Vietnamese mother, but her American schoolmates taunt her with the nickname "pajamas." Will Ut ever be accepted in her new home? This book teaches children about accepting differences in each other. Featured on PBS "Reading Rainbow."

Ward, Leila. *I Am Eyes, Ni Macho.* New York: Scholastic, 1978.

A young African child describes all that can be seen in the beautiful environment, thereby teaching young children what Africa looks like while exploring the visual sense. This lovely picture book can act as a springboard for picture books created by your preschoolers to describe their own neighborhood.

Williams, Jay. *Everyone Knows What a Dragon Looks Like.* New York: Four Winds Press, 1976.

In this Chinese tale a young boy befriends a sweet old man who's really a dragon—a symbol of good luck.

Yolen, Jane. *The Emperor and the Kite.* Cleveland, OH: World Publishing, 1967.

Djeow Seow is the tiny fourth daughter of the emperor. No one pays any attention to her and she is very lonely. But later, her smallness proves to be an asset—especially when evil men threaten the kingdom.

Young, Ed. *Lon Po Po.* New York: Scholastic, 1989.

Ed Young's poignant illustrations make this "Little Red Riding Hood" story from China a powerful offering.

Nonfiction

Bernheim, Marc and Evelyne. *In Africa.* New York: Atheneum, 1973.

Black and white photos introduce children to the continent with jungles, deserts, mountains, great plains, and so much more.

Feelings, Muriel. *Jambo Means Hello.* New York: Dial Press, 1974.

This Caldecott Honor alphabet book offers a globally enriching experience as it introduces 24 Swahili words with wonderful illustrations of important aspects of traditional East Africa life. Featured on PBS "Reading Rainbow."

Martin, Patricia Miles. *The Rice Bowl Pet.* New York: Thomas Y. Crowell, 1962.

Ah Jim describes what a typical day is like in Chinatown—his very own neighborhood.

Musgrove, Margaret. *Ashanti to Zulu.* New York: Dial Books for Young Readers, 1977.

Here's another alphabet book that teaches children about African traditions. A Caldecott Medal winner.

Spier, Peter. *People.* New York: Doubleday, 1980.

This book tells in wonderful pictures that there are four billion human beings on earth. They come in all sizes, shapes, and colors, but they all want the same things—to look beautiful, to have shelter, and so forth. Also available in Big Book format.

Waters, Kate and Madeline Slovenz-Low. *Lion Dancer.* New York: Scholastic, 1990.

This informative photo book presents Ernie Wan's experiences on Chinese New Year. Ernie performs his first Lion Dance and the story tells how he prepares for the big event.

Global Snacktime

Bread Friends Around the World

Cut pieces of bread (white, rye, and wheat) into "gingerbread" people using a cookie cutter. Paint on features using milk that has one or two drops of food coloring added to it. If desired, toast bread people and enjoy with juice or milk.

Teacher note: Food painting requires brand new, washed brushes. After they are used on bread, you can wash them and use for tempera painting.

Global Game

Flag Matching

This matching game will help children learn shapes and colors while also introducing the flags of many nations. Make copies of the Flags reproducibles (see next two pages). Color as directed (parts with no color remain white). Tape together a few copies to serve as game boards. Cut other copies into squares to be matched with the boards. Laminate all with clear Contact paper for durability.

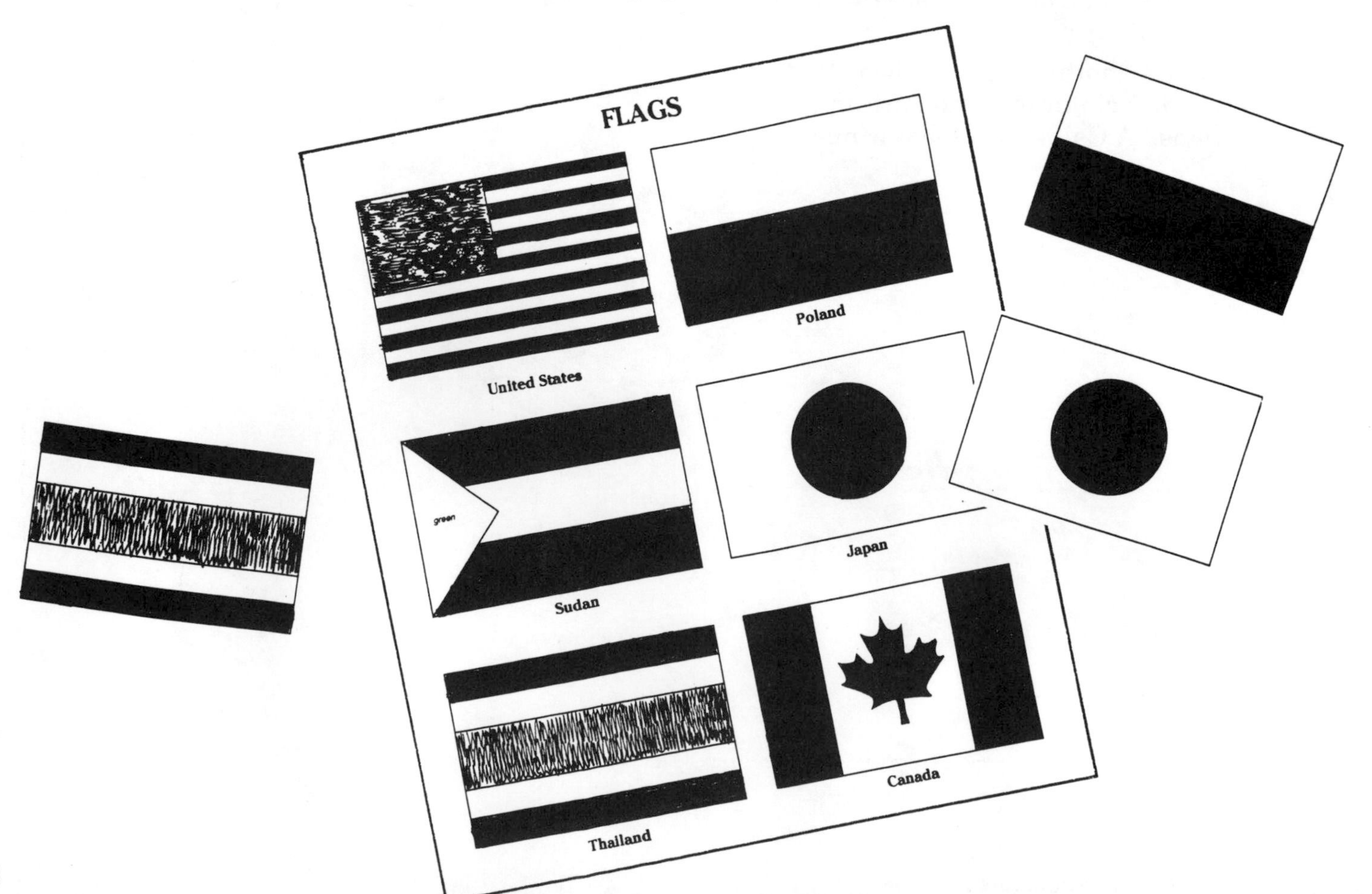

Flags

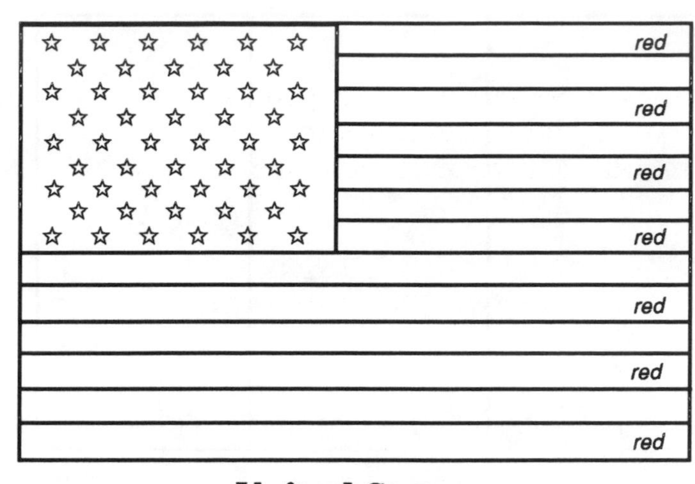

United States

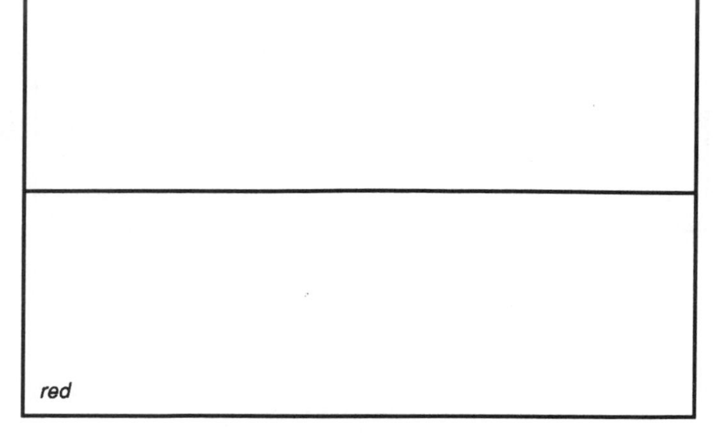

Poland

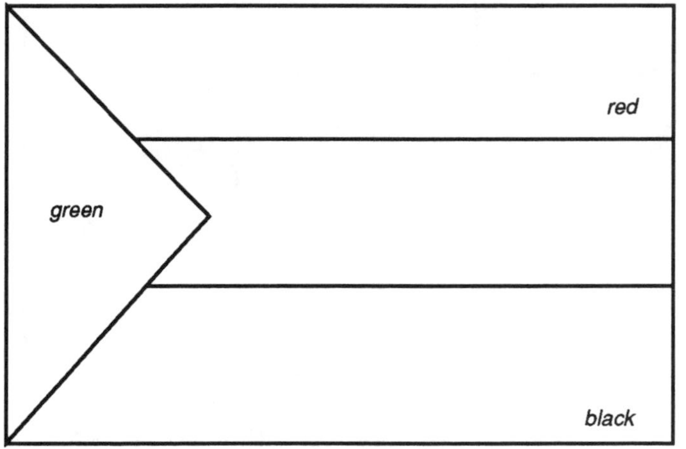

Sudan

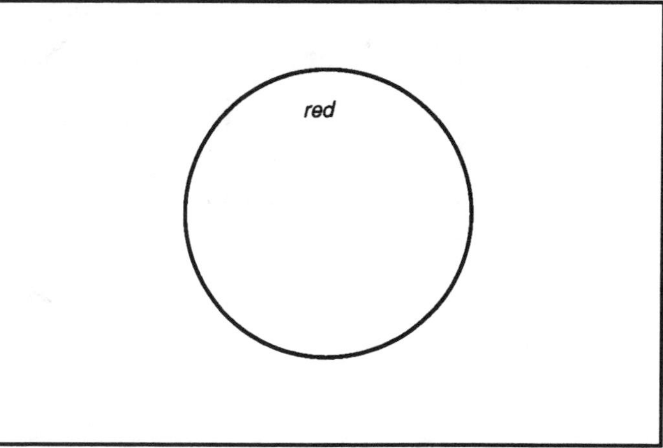

Japan

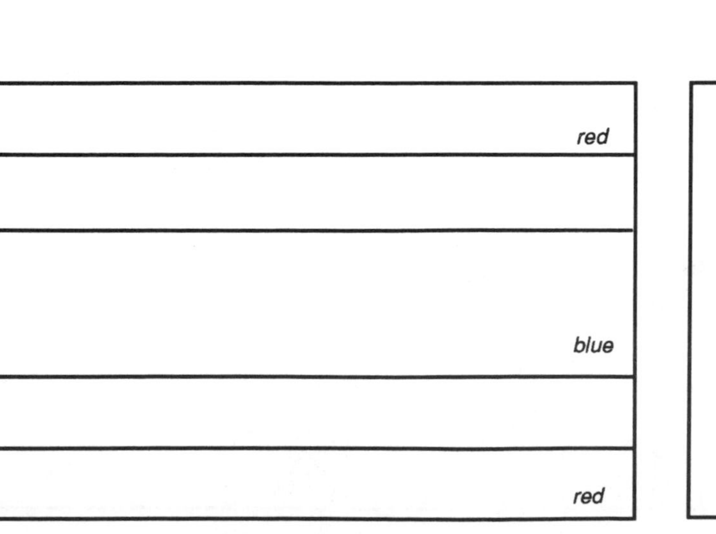

Thailand

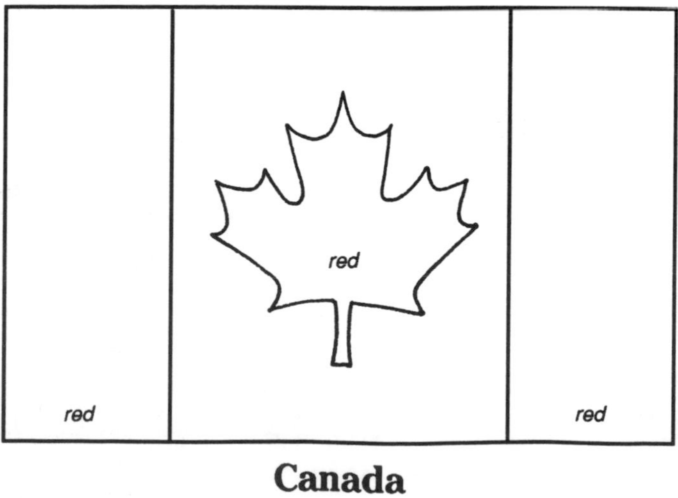

Canada

Flags

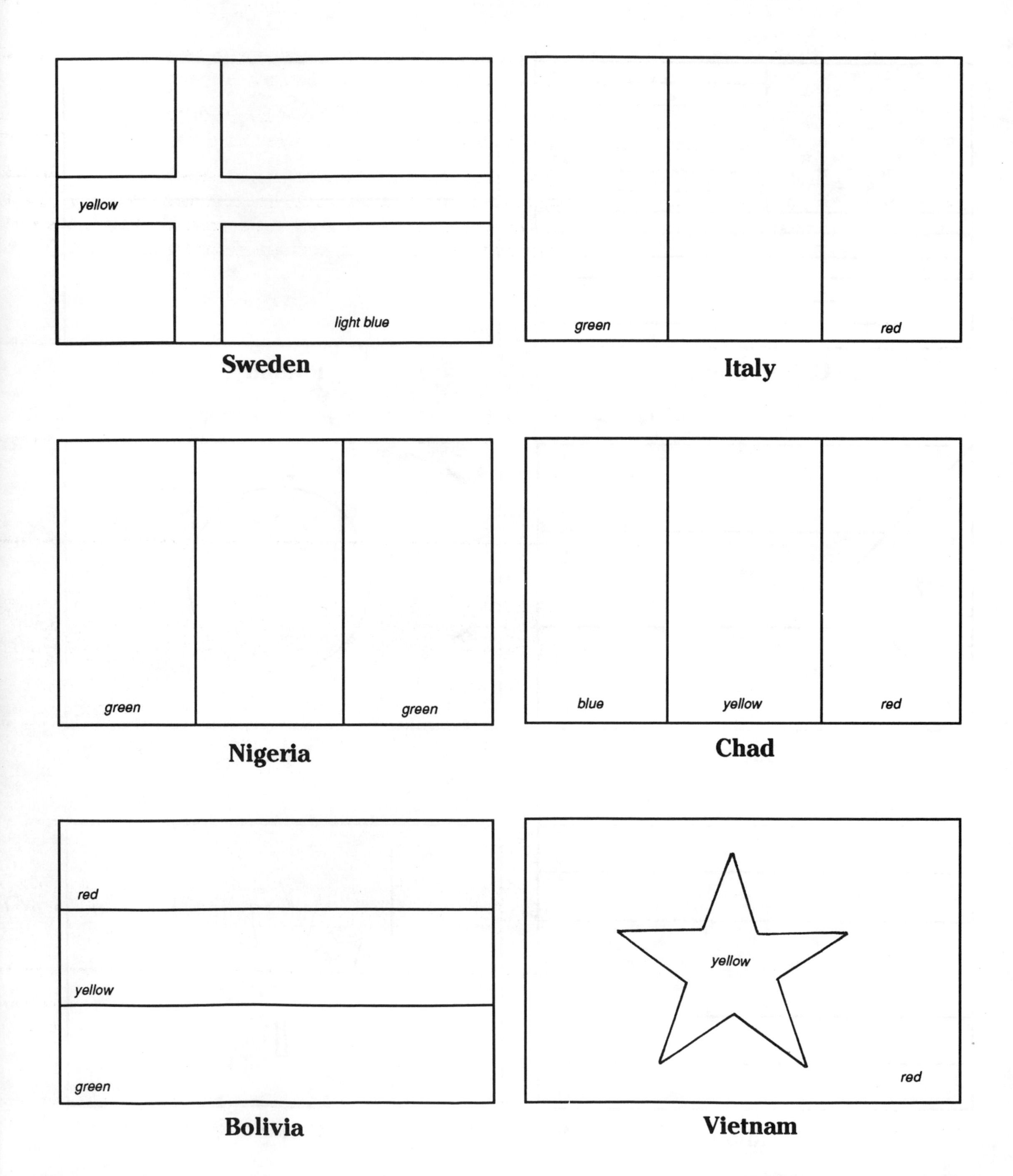
yellow
light blue
Sweden
green
red
Italy
green
green
Nigeria
blue
yellow
red
Chad
red
yellow
green
Bolivia
yellow
red
Vietnam